AISLE BE THERE FOR YOU

FOR YOU

Every Bride's Best Friend

Shazia Ahmed

Dedication

To my incredible parents, Aftab Ahmed and Mehtab Begum, whose unwavering love, support, and wisdom have shaped me into the person I am today. Your belief in me has been my greatest strength, and I am forever grateful for the values you've instilled in me.

And to my three beautiful children, Aliya, Alisha, and Ali—my greatest joys and constant inspirations. You fill my life with love, laughter, and purpose, and remind me every day of the beauty in life's simplest moments. This book is for you.

Contents

Contents

Foreword

Hi there! We're Aliya and Alisha—proud to say we're the children of a supermom who just happens to be one of India's most amazing wedding planners. But wait—it gets even better. Not only has she helped hundreds of brides plan their dream weddings, but now, she's written a book! Yup, you're holding *Aisle Be There for You,* the ultimate guide for brides-to-be. And while we might be her biggest fans, we promise our mom didn't bribe us to write this. (Well, maybe a little ice cream was involved...)

Growing up with our mom, Shazia Ahmed, has been a ride—an absolutely fabulous one. If you think planning a wedding is hard, try living in a house where every day feels like an event! We've watched our mom pour her heart into planning weddings, always making sure that each couple's day is not just special but personal, unique, and unforgettable.

Aliya: "Mom's superpower is making people feel heard. When she plans a wedding, it's like she magically knows exactly what the bride wants, even if she doesn't say it out loud. I think that's why every wedding she plans feels so personal and perfect."

Alisha: "Yeah, and she's always telling brides to 'just be themselves', which I think is great advice. She says weddings are about celebrating love but also about celebrating the couple's story. That's pretty cool, don't you think?"

As kids, we've seen more weddings than most people our age—no, seriously. Our lives have been a whirlwind of bridal fittings, wedding decor, and food tastings. We can tell you the difference between ivory and eggshell white (yes, there is a difference) and spot a good DJ from a mile away. Our mom has made us experts in wedding trivia, whether we wanted to be or not!

But here's the thing—through all those weddings, we've learned some pretty important lessons from our mom. She's always saying that weddings are just the beginning, not the end. The big day is exciting, but it's the love and the partnership that follow that really matter. That's why she's all about helping brides create a day that reflects their unique journey.

Aliya: "I think my favourite part of Mom's passion is how she always finds a way to make every wedding different. One time, she planned a beach wedding where the couple walked down the aisle barefoot. Another time, she helped plan this

huge Bollywood-themed wedding with tons of colours and dancers. It's always something new and exciting!"

Alisha: "And mom always says, 'Don't sweat the small stuff.' She's helped brides handle last-minute dress disasters, unexpected rainstorms, and even a piece of missing wedding jewellery once. She stays calm no matter what and just rolls with it. I think that's why brides trust her so much.

Plus, she's pretty fun to be around. Brides always seem so happy when they're with her. She has this way of making people feel relaxed even when they're stressed out. And let me tell you, brides can get really stressed out!"

This book is like a sneak peek into everything we've seen our mom do for years. It's packed with all her best advice, funny stories (trust us, she has a lot of those!), and super practical tips that will help any bride plan her big day with confidence. Whether you're just starting to plan your wedding or you're already knee-deep in invite lists and colour schemes, *Aisle Be There for You* has something for you.

And the best part? Our mom isn't about telling you what you should do. She's all about giving you options and ideas so that you can create a wedding that's as unique as you are. She's helped so many brides turn their dreams into reality, and now she's sharing all her secrets with you. We can't wait for you to dive into this book and see just how amazing it is!

So, to all the brides out there, we hope this book helps you feel inspired, excited, and ready to plan the wedding of your dreams. And just remember, no matter what, you've got this—and our mom's got your back! Trust us, she's pretty good at what she does.

Now, go ahead, turn the page, and let's start planning that dream wedding!

Introduction

If you've found yourself here, with this book nestled in your hands or glowing on your screen, take a deep breath because you, my friend, are at the PERFECT place! Whether you're a bride-to-be with dreams in your eyes, a doting family member who can't wait to dance at the sangeet, or a curious cat with a wedding to attend, you're about to embark on a journey through the magnificent world of Indian weddings.

Are your insides doing the jitterbug at the mere thought of planning a wedding? The elaborate rituals, the glimmering outfits, the tantalising food, the larger-than-life celebrations—we know it can feel like learning to juggle while riding a unicycle. Fret not, because this book is your friendly companion and guide to navigating the grandeur, the traditions, and the little details of Indian weddings with flair and grace.

Let's wind back the clock a little. A couple of decades ago, Indian weddings were mostly about close-knit family affairs with a sprinkle of tradition and homemade sweets. The dulcet tones of folk songs, the scent of marigold garlands, and the hum of age-old rituals created a tapestry of warmth and affection.

Fast forward to today, and you'll find a panorama of splendour, creativity, and, sometimes, fairytale extravaganzas. The wedding industry has evolved into a multi-billion dollar market. From luxurious venues that would make palaces seem quaint, celebrity performers who set the stage on fire, to destination weddings in exotic locales – the options are endless and only limited by one's imagination.

Now, you might ask, what changed? Well, Indian weddings started to put on their travelling boots and global hats. With the world shrinking into a global village, our beloved Indian weddings extended their roots and branched out, embracing elements from around the world.

Add to this mix the wonders of the internet! Social media platforms are now the new 'baraats', arriving with trends, inspirations, and a flood of information. Your Instagram and Pinterest are brimming with ideas, and it's like having a wedding planner in your pocket.

Weddings are a momentous occasion for many people, and some begin saving up for the big day from a very young age. From setting aside pennies in jars to opening bank accounts specifically for the purpose of wedding savings, couples often take financial planning into account when planning their special day.

But with all this magnificence comes its own set of dilemmas. How do you choose the right wedding planner? Which photographer can capture your moments like they're straight out of a fairytale? How do you curate a menu that leaves people licking their fingers? And how, oh how, do you manage to keep the essence of traditions alive amidst all the glitter?

Through the pages of this book, we'll dance through the best ways to choose destinations and venues that feel like they were created just for you. We'll saunter through options for outfits that'll make you feel regal. We'll sip on tips on how to create a menu that's the talk of the town. And we'll hold hands as we find ways to keep traditions close to our hearts while embracing the new.

But wait, that's not all! We'll be your confidant in helping you with not just the big decisions; we've also got your back with the nitty-gritty. From selecting the perfect wedding invitations to ensuring the logistical pieces fall into place like a harmonious symphony, we're here for you.

In this book, every page turned is a step closer to creating your own slice of magic. Together, let's weave dreams with threads of tradition and wings of modernity. Let's make your wedding not just a day but a timeless memory, an artwork to be cherished forever.

Chapter 1

Dream Wedding Decoded

Oh, the excitement of the big day! The day you've probably dreamed of since you first saw those Bollywood lovebirds singing in the rain. Now it's your turn, and the sheer thought is like a roller coaster of emotions. But wait, where do you even begin? There's just so much to do! The thought of planning an Indian wedding can feel like being a maestro trying to conduct an orchestra for the first time – but without the baton. And instead of violins and cellos, you've got caterers and decorators waiting for your cue. If you're worried, you're not alone in feeling overwhelmed. Indian weddings are like a multi-tiered cake, and each tier comes with its own set of sweet and sticky tasks. There's the venue to select, the caterer to choose, the guest list to compile, the outfits to pick, and not to forget the traditions and rituals to adhere to.

This is exactly where we step in to give you that metaphorical baton and guide you through orchestrating your own grand symphony.

Let's get down to brass tacks. A trusty checklist is your best friend. Think of it as a magical carpet that will carry you gracefully through this adventurous ride. Grab a notebook, or fire up that wedding planning app because we are about to create the ultimate checklist!

Discovering Your Wedding's True Direction

Before anything else, the key is to find your wedding's 'true north.' You need to decide what kind of wedding you wish to have. Is it going to be a cosy, intimate gathering or a grand royal procession? Do you want a traditional ceremony or a fusion of old and new? Conversations with your partner and families are pivotal in shaping this vision.

Budget Allocation

Jot down a clear budget and allocate percentages to major categories like venue, outfits, decor, food, and photography.

Venue & Dates

- List your preferred wedding dates.
- Make a shortlist of venues that align with your vision and budget.
- Contact venues for availability and pricing.
- Finalise and book your wedding venue.

Outfits & Attire

- Decide on your wedding trousseau – this includes all your outfits for different ceremonies.

- If you're getting anything custom-made, make sure to leave ample time for fittings and alterations.
- Don't forget about matching accessories and footwear!

Decor & Theme

- Decide on a theme for your wedding.
- Shortlist and contact decorators.
- Finalise decor elements like flowers, lights, and centrepieces.

Catering & Menu

- Research and shortlist caterers.
- Decide on the style of food – traditional, continental, or a mix.
- Attend tastings and finalise the menu.

Photography & Videography

- Research photographers and videographers.
- Look through portfolios and shortlist your favourites.
- Finalise and book your photography and videography team.

Entertainment & Music

- Decide on the kind of entertainment you want – DJ, live band, traditional musicians.
- Book the entertainment well in advance.

Miscellaneous

- Arrange transportation for guests if needed.
- Choose and order wedding favours.
- Plan pre-wedding functions like Mehendi, Sangeet, and others.
- Set up a gift registry if you have one.

Taking Care of Yourself

- Amidst all the hustle, don't forget to take care of yourself.
- Plan your pre-wedding beauty regimen.
- Take time to relax and de-stress.

Remember, dear reader, while this checklist is here to keep you grounded and organised, it's also meant to be flexible. Don't be afraid to tweak it, customise it, and make it your own. This checklist is not set in stone, but rather, it's like a fluid melody that changes and evolves as you get closer to your wedding day.

Alright, let's cut to the chase! It's time to roll up our sleeves and dive into the details. The upcoming chapters are your toolbox, your secret weapon in tackling each item on our checklist.

We're talking concrete tips and tricks. From finding the perfect venue that's got the "wow" factor to picking outfits that will make jaws drop. Wondering what to serve to tickle

those taste buds? We've got you covered. Puzzling over the perfect playlist for the night? Consider it sorted.

And it's not just about the shiny stuff. We're also talking real talk on traditions – which ones you might want to keep, how to give them a modern twist, and what you can do to make them uniquely yours.

Looking for that perfect destination wedding? We'll walk you through the best spots and dish out the details on how to make it work without breaking the bank.

In short, every chapter is going to be a deep dive into making each part of your wedding not just work but work spectacularly. This is the nitty-gritty, the down and dirty, the ultimate guide to making your wedding absolutely unforgettable.

So, keep those pages turning because we've got a lot to cover and no time to waste. Let's do this!

Chapter 2

Money Matters: The Wedding Budget

Alright, let's talk about the elephant in the room – money! Yeah, it might not be the most romantic topic, but let's face it, the budget is what makes the wedding world go round. So, let's grab the bull by the horns and dive into the art of drafting a realistic budget that doesn't make your wallet run for the hills.

Breaking The Chains: The Evolution of Wedding Budgets

To understand where we stand today, let's take a quick stroll down memory lane. Once upon a time, weddings were all about maintaining the status quo. Families would often go out of their way to match their societal stature, and unfortunately, this sometimes came with the heavy burden of dowry – where major chunks of the budget went into gold, cars, and gifts. It was more materialistic and less about the couple.

Fast forward to now, and the winds of change are blowing! Gen Z couples are breaking the chains. They're not too concerned about societal norms, and there's a growing aversion to the dowry system. The focus is now on celebrating love and making cherished memories.

What's more, modern couples often don't want to burden their parents. Many of today's lovebirds are financially independent and want to contribute to their wedding expenses.

Know The Market, Save Your Pockets

This is important: if you walk directly into the jaws of the vendors, chances are you might get bitten! Those folks can sometimes really mark up their prices. But guess what? A wedding planner knows the lay of the land. They can be your ally in getting you the real deals. Think of them as your financial Indiana Jones, exploring the market jungle for you!

Understanding Wedding Budget Spectrum

Think of weddings like cars – you can get a trusty Maruti or a luxurious Mercedes. The more moolah you invest, the more oomph you get. But here's the thing: a limited budget doesn't mean your wedding can't be fabulous. It's all about smart allocation and knowing where to splurge and where to save.

Must-Haves vs Good-to-Haves

This is your North Star when drafting a budget. It's essential to differentiate between what's non-negotiable and what's a nice add-on. Everyone's priorities are different. Some folks want a 5-star venue and are willing to go easy on other aspects, while others dream of lavish decor in open spaces like farmhouses, where they can craft magical experiences.

There's also the staunch believer in exclusive vendors: those who won't settle for anyone but their favourite photographers and makeup artists. And let's not forget about those who want to create an unforgettable night with artists, singers, and performers.

So, how do you do this? Sit down with your partner and make two lists: "Must-Haves" and "Good-to-Haves." This will help you laser-focus on what's critical for you and where you can be flexible.

In the next section, we'll talk about how to allocate your funds to different elements based on your priorities. Stay tuned because we're about to get into the nitty-gritty of making your budget work like a charm!

Allocating Funds to Different Elements

So, you've got your budget and your "Must-Haves" and "Good-to-Haves" lists sorted. Now, it's time for some action! It's like building a puzzle, where every piece has its place. Let's learn how to allocate your funds smartly across different aspects of your wedding without sacrificing the oomph.

Hierarchy of Allocation

Generally, there's a pecking order in terms of budget allocation. Here's a typical ranking from the higher to lower end of the expense spectrum:

- Property (venue)
- Decor
- Food and Beverage
- Artists/Entertainment
- Logistics
- Hospitality

Of course, this hierarchy might change based on your "Must-Haves."

- **Property: The Setting of Your Tale**

The venue is usually one of the biggest chunks of your budget. If having a specific type of venue is on your "Must-Have" list, then this is where a significant part of your treasure will go. Whether it's a royal palace or a serene beach, make sure it resonates with your dream.

- ## Decor: Crafting the Ambiance

The decor sets the mood for your wedding. If you dream of a fairytale setting or a Bollywood extravaganza, then you need to carve out a sizeable portion for decor. Keep in mind that creativity and DIY can work wonders if you're tight on the budget!

- ## Food & Beverage: A Feast for the Senses

Let's be honest, years down the line, people might not remember the decor, but they'll remember the food. It's often a good idea not to skimp on this part. But again, if this is more of a "Good-to-Have", then you can be clever with menu choices without compromising quality.

- ## Artists/Entertainment: The Life of The Party

Are you the couple that wants the dance floor packed and the crowd grooving all night? If so, this is where you don't want to pinch pennies. But remember, entertainment doesn't always mean big names; sometimes, local bands or DJs can rock the house just as well.

- ## Logistics: The Backbone

This involves everything that makes your wedding run smoothly transportation, lighting, sound systems, etc. Don't overlook this, as it's the backbone of your event. Make sure you allocate enough to ensure things run like a well-oiled machine.

- ### Hospitality: Rolling out the Red Carpet

Last but not least, hospitality. This is all about how you take care of your guests. Depending on your style, this could be as simple as ensuring comfortable seating or as lavish as personal butlers for each guest.

- ### Be Flexible and Adaptive

Remember, this is just a guide. Your wedding is a personal expression of your love story. Don't be afraid to move things around to match what really matters to you.

In the next section, we will explore clever ways to save without compromising on your dream wedding. Because, let's face it, who doesn't love some savvy saving tricks? Onward we go!

Clever Ways to Save Without Compromising on the Dream

Alright, let's get crafty! Who said you can't have your wedding cake and eat it too? In this section, we'll dish out some clever hacks to keep your pockets happy while still living the dream. Buckle up because we're about to save like a boss!

1. Early Bird Gets the Worm

Start your wedding preparations early. You'll have more options, and you'll be in a better position to snag those early-bird discounts. Venues, caterers, and even decorators often offer discounts for bookings made well in advance.

2. Off-Peak Magic

Consider having your wedding during the off-peak season or on a weekday. The demand is lower, and so are the prices. Plus, it's likely that your venue will be less crowded and more exclusive.

3. Double Up with a Venue

Choose a venue that's a package deal – a place that is beautiful as is and requires minimal decor. Better yet, pick a place that can host both the ceremony and reception. This cuts down on transportation costs and can often get you a package deal.

4. Food Finesse

Go for a plated dinner instead of a buffet; it often turns out cheaper. Be smart with the menu choices. Pick a few exquisite items instead of an extensive menu. And don't forget local and seasonal ingredients are your friends!

5. DIY Decor Diva

Unleash your inner creative genius. Pinterest and YouTube are your allies. From invitation cards to table centrepieces, there's a world of classy DIY options that can add a personal touch without breaking the bank.

6. Negotiation is an Art

Don't be shy to haggle. Vendors often have wiggle room in pricing. Be polite but firm. Let them know you're considering other options, and they might just sweeten the deal for you.

7. Harness the Power of Social Media

Reach out on social media for recommendations. Sometimes, your network can connect you with amazing deals and undiscovered talents who can add that special touch to your wedding without the hefty price tag.

8. The Friend Squad

Got friends who are photographers, makeup artists, or DJs? Don't hesitate to ask them if they'd like to offer their services as a wedding gift. It adds a personal touch and can save a pretty penny.

9. Keep an Eye on Extras

It's the little things that add up. Keep an eye on the extras – do you really need that chocolate fountain or the ice sculpture? Be judicious with the add-ons.

10. Smart Attire Choices

Rent or tailor-make your wedding attire instead of going for designer labels. These days, renting exquisite wedding dresses and suits is in vogue and kinder to the wallet.

Remember, at the end of the day, it's about celebrating love with your nearest and dearest. With a bit of ingenuity and clever planning, you can have a day that's both magical and budget-friendly.

WEDDING BUDGET

CEREMONY 1
(HALDI/MEHENDI)

DESCRIPTION	AMOUNT

CEREMONY 2
(SANGEETH)

DESCRIPTION	AMOUNT

TOTAL SPENT

REMAINING

WEDDING BUDGET

CEREMONY 3 (SHAADI/NIKAH)

DESCRIPTION	AMOUNT

CEREMONY 4 (RECEPTION/VALIMA)

DESCRIPTION	AMOUNT

TOTAL SPENT

REMAINING

WEDDING BUDGET

BRIDE'S FAMILY

GROOM & BRIDE

VENUE

DESCRIPTION	AMOUNT

FOOD & BEVERAGES

DESCRIPTION	AMOUNT

TOTAL SPENT

REMAINING

WEDDING BUDGET

GROOM'S FAMILY

BRIDE'S FAMILY

GROOM & BRIDE

DECORATIONS

DESCRIPTION	AMOUNT

OUTFITS

DESCRIPTION	AMOUNT

TOTAL SPENT

REMAINING

● TO START   ✓ OK   → DELAY   ✓ STUCK   ✗ CANCEL

WEDDING BUDGET

DESCRIPTION	AMOUNT

Chapter 3

The Celebrity Wedding Effect: Celebrity Style, Influence, and Personalisation

Celebrity weddings have long captivated the public's imagination. These grand events often serve as a reflection of the personalities and tastes of the stars involved, setting trends that ripple through society. When influential people tie the knot, they don't just create memorable moments for themselves; they also leave a lasting impact on the world of weddings. This chapter delves into how celebrities infuse their personal style into their weddings, the trends they set, and the critical importance of personalisation in making a wedding truly unique.

The Art of Personalisation in Celebrity Weddings

Personalisation is at the heart of any memorable wedding, and celebrities are masters at incorporating their distinct styles into their special day. Unlike traditional weddings that may follow more conventional norms, celebrity weddings often break the mould, offering a window into the couple's world.

1. Venue Selection:

The choice of venue is a significant element where personal style shines. Celebrities often select locations that hold personal significance or align with their aesthetic preferences. For instance, George Clooney and Amal Alamuddin's wedding in Venice was not only a nod to the city's romantic ambiance but also a reflection of the couple's love for history and art. On the other hand, Kim Kardashian and Kanye West's opulent wedding at the historic Forte di Belvedere in Florence was a grand declaration of their larger-than-life personas. Celebrity couple Anushka Sharma and Virat Kohli, known as "Virushka", chose Borgo Finocchieto in Tuscany, while Priyanka Chopra and Nick Jonas chose Umaid Bhawan Palace in Jodhpur, Rajasthan.

2. Fashion Statements:

Fashion is another arena where celebrities make bold statements. The bridal attire often becomes iconic, influencing bridal fashion trends for years to come. When Meghan Markle married Prince Harry, her choice of a minimalist Givenchy gown designed by Clare Waight Keller became an instant classic, emphasising simplicity and elegance over excessive embellishment. Conversely, Priyanka Chopra's wedding to Nick Jonas featured a custom

Ralph Lauren gown with a 75-foot veil, showcasing a blend of traditional and contemporary styles that honoured her Indian heritage while appealing to Western tastes.

3. Custom Elements and Decor:

From bespoke invitations to personalised decor, celebrities ensure that every detail of their wedding reflects their style. Beyoncé and Jay-Z's wedding was reportedly decorated with 70,000 white orchids flown in from Thailand, highlighting their preference for grandeur and exclusivity. Meanwhile, Blake Lively and Ryan Reynolds opted for a more intimate and rustic setting, with handwritten vows and a dessert table laden with Southern treats, showcasing their down-to-earth charm and love for home comforts.

The Importance of Personalisation in Weddings:

Personalisation is not just a trend but a critical element in making any wedding truly special. It's what turns a standard event into a deeply meaningful celebration that reflects the couple's journey, values, and dreams.

1. Creating Unique Memories:

Personalised weddings create unique memories that resonate deeply with the couple and their guests. When a wedding is tailored to reflect the personalities of the bride and groom, it stands out and becomes memorable. For example, a couple who loves adventure might choose a

mountaintop ceremony, which not only provides a stunning backdrop but also tells a story about their shared passions.

2. Reflecting Values and Beliefs:

Incorporating personal elements into a wedding also allows couples to reflect their values and beliefs. Whether it's through the inclusion of cultural traditions, personalised vows, or charitable donations in lieu of favours, these elements ensure that the wedding is a true reflection of who the couple is.

3. Enhancing Guest Experience:

Personalisation can significantly enhance the guest experience. When guests see elements that are distinctly "you", it makes them feel more connected to the celebration. Personalised touches such as custom welcome bags, personalised thank-you notes, or interactive elements like photo booths with props that reflect the couple's interests can make guests feel appreciated and involved.

4. Legacy and Inspiration:

A personalised wedding also leaves a legacy and can inspire others. When a wedding truly reflects the couple, it can serve as inspiration for others to think outside the box and personalise their own weddings. The wedding of Prince William and Kate Middleton, with its blend of tradition and personal touches, has inspired countless couples to find

ways to incorporate their own histories and stories into their ceremonies.

A Masterclass in Personal Style and Luxury: Ambani Weddings

The Ambani wedding, a union that united two of India's most influential families, was a spectacle of grandeur and opulence. Known for their lavish lifestyle and significant contributions to various industries, the Ambanis left no stone unturned to ensure that the wedding was a reflection of their status, culture, and personal style.

What are the biggest takeaways for you to make your wedding as good as the Ambani wedding?

Fashion Statements and Cultural Fusion

The Ambani wedding set new benchmarks in bridal fashion and attire. The bride's ensembles were a harmonious blend of traditional Indian craftsmanship and contemporary design, reflecting their personal style and cultural heritage. Each outfit was meticulously crafted by renowned designers, featuring intricate embroidery, handwoven fabrics, and precious jewels that exemplified the richness of Indian textile arts.

They are not just outfits; they are a reflection of your style and personality. Make your outfits a reflection of YOU!

Personalised Touches and Cultural Rituals

Despite the grandeur, the Ambani wedding did not lose sight of personalisation and cultural significance. The ceremonies were steeped in traditional rituals that honoured the couple's heritage and values. Each ritual was performed with utmost reverence, ensuring that the spiritual essence of the wedding was preserved amidst the opulence.

Personalised touches were evident throughout the celebrations. Custom-made invitations, bespoke gifts for guests, and personalised decor elements created a warm and intimate atmosphere. The family's attention to detail in incorporating these personal elements demonstrated that even in a wedding of such scale, it is the thoughtful, individualised touches that make the event truly special.

Setting Trends and Leaving a Legacy:

For couples around the world, these celebrity weddings serve as a source of inspiration, showcasing the importance of personalisation, cultural respect, and attention to detail. It highlights that while grandeur and opulence can make a wedding visually stunning, it is the personal and cultural elements that imbue it with lasting significance and emotional resonance.

A wedding is more than just a union of two individuals; it is a celebration of love, heritage, and personal style on an unprecedented scale. It stands as a masterclass in how to create a wedding that is not only a spectacle of luxury but also a deeply personal and meaningful celebration.

Celebrity weddings are more than just lavish events; they are showcases of personal style and sources of inspiration. By incorporating unique elements that reflect their personalities, celebrities set trends and demonstrate the importance of personalisation in creating a memorable wedding. For anyone planning their big day, looking to these high-profile weddings can provide ideas and encouragement to infuse their own special touches. In the end, a wedding that truly represents the couple is one that will be remembered and cherished for a lifetime.

Trends Inspired by Celebrity Weddings:

Let's dive into some of the major trends set by recent high-profile weddings.

- **Destination Weddings:**

Inspired by celebrities, more and more Indian couples are opting for destination weddings. These weddings combine the charm of an exotic location with the intimacy of a close-knit affair. While international locations like Italy and the Maldives are popular, picturesque locations in India, such as Rajasthan, Goa, and Kerala, are equally sought-after.

- **Fusion of Cultures:**

A blend of Indian and Western traditions is the new trend that is here to stay. This multicultural trend has inspired many couples, especially those from different cultural backgrounds, to celebrate their love by embracing both cultures equally.

- **Unconventional Bridal Wear:**

From sneakers under the lehenga to wearing white or pastels, brides are encouraged to experiment with their wedding outfits. The idea is to break away from traditional reds and maroons and choose colours and styles that reflect their personality.

- **Personalisation:**

Deepika Padukone's saree featuring 'Sada Saubhagyavati Bhava' embroidery, which means 'be forever fortunate' in Sanskrit, was a touching personal touch. This sparked a trend of adding personalised elements to wedding attire or decor, adding a unique touch to the wedding.

- **Social Media Engagement:**

The hashtags that took over social media during these star-studded affairs have now caught on. Many couples are creating their unique wedding hashtags for guests to use and sharing personalised wedding albums on social media platforms.

Pinterest vs. Reality Syndrome

As we marvel at the influence of celebrity weddings, it's important to segue into a phenomenon that often accompanies these inspirations: the "Pinterest vs. Reality Syndrome." This is where the dreams inspired by high-profile nuptials meet the practical world of wedding planning.

I recall a client who once approached me with a bright, vivaciously coloured Pinterest image of a table setting adorned with a variety of flowers native to a completely different continent. The task seemed simple to them: recreate this vision within their chosen venue. However, this request came laden with unspoken challenges. Firstly, their budget did not stretch to accommodate the exotic opulence they aspired to. Secondly, the photo was taken in an outdoor setting with natural lighting that enhanced the vibrancy of the colours—a stark contrast to the indoor venue they had booked.

This delicate situation is one that wedding planners often navigate. While it's easy to fall in love with polished images of lush floral arrangements and ethereal settings, the reality of geographical, budgetary, and logistical constraints can be sobering. For instance, the low ceilings of a charming local hall cannot morph to accommodate the grand chandeliers seen in a grand ballroom with vaulted ceilings.

The heart of the matter is that while aspirations are boundless, reality requires a grounding in practicality. It's a balancing act between managing expectations and delivering the most magical experience within the given parameters.

Amid the glitz and glamour of celebrity weddings and the cascading effect of their wedding trends, it's crucial to remember that a wedding is a celebration of love and commitment between two individuals. Every couple is different, with unique tastes and preferences.

Chapter 4

Location, Location, Location!

"Where it happens matters as much as what happens," a quote that perfectly encapsulates the essence of our next topic of discussion: wedding venues. Undoubtedly, the choice of the wedding venue lays the foundation for the overall wedding experience. Whether it's an opulent palace echoing the grandeur of royal weddings or a tranquil beach adding a touch of serene elegance to the nuptials, the venue is much more than just a location. It sets the tone for your wedding, reflecting your personal style and love story while also providing the backdrop against which your special memories will be etched.

In this chapter, we delve into the journey of selecting the perfect venue for your dream wedding. We'll begin by discussing your vision and crystallising it to estimate the guest count — two critical starting points for venue selection. Next, we'll explore other crucial factors that can make or break your venue decision, such as location, available amenities, and venue policies.

Selecting the perfect wedding venue may appear overwhelming at first, but with proper guidance and a clear vision, it can become one of the most thrilling highlights of your wedding planning journcy. So, let us embark on this adventure and create the perfect setting for your enchanting day.

Determining Your Vision and Guest Count:

As you embark on the path to selecting your wedding venue, it's important to first establish your vision and have a rough estimate of your guest count. These two factors act as the guiding light in your venue selection journey, helping you narrow down options and tailor your choice to best fit your needs.

Vision for the Event:

The first step in venue selection is to have a clear understanding of your vision for the event. Your vision is an extension of your and your partner's personalities, preferences, and dreams, encapsulating the look, feel, and flow you desire for your wedding.

Do you envision a grand royal affair, a simple garden ceremony, or perhaps a beach wedding? Is your style more classic and traditional or modern and minimalist? Do you want an indoor event, an outdoor event, or a mix of both? Is there a particular theme or colour scheme you wish to incorporate?

Having clarity on these aspects can significantly streamline your venue search. For example, if you've always dreamed of a beach wedding, you can immediately rule out city ballrooms or mountain resorts. Similarly, if you're planning a winter wedding and want to ensure comfort for your guests, an indoor venue might be more appropriate.

Guest Count:

The next crucial factor to consider is your guest count. Having an estimated number of guests not only helps determine the size of the venue you'll need but also impacts your budget and venue choice.

It's important to remember that the number of guests you invite directly influences the cost of your wedding. More guests mean more food, beverages, seating arrangements, invitations, and possibly a larger, more expensive venue.

It's also worth noting that not all venues can accommodate all sizes of guest lists. Some venues may be too small for a large gathering, while others may be too large for an intimate celebration, which could make the event feel sparse and lack warmth.

Estimate your guest count before you start looking at venues. This doesn't have to be an exact number but a reasonable range. This will help you filter out venues that are too small or large for your guest count, saving you time and preventing potential disappointments later on.

I have provided a sample guest list template at the end of this chapter, which you can refer to.

Factors to Consider: Location, Amenities, and Venue Policies

Once you've established your vision and estimated your guest count, there are several other important factors to consider when selecting a venue. The right venue should not only align with your vision and accommodate your guests but also provide the necessary amenities and agree with your event policies. Let's delve into these aspects in detail.

Location:

The location of your venue plays a pivotal role in setting the tone of your wedding and can significantly impact your guests' experience. It should be easily accessible and convenient for the majority of your guests. If you have a lot of out-of-town guests, you might want to consider venues close to hotels or airports.

When selecting a location, think about the vibe you want to create. If you envision a rustic, relaxed wedding, a vineyard or barn might be the perfect fit. For a more formal, elegant affair, a grand ballroom or historic estate could be more suitable.

Amenities:

The available amenities at the venue are also crucial considerations. Check if the venue has essentials such as restrooms, changing rooms, and parking spaces. If you're considering an outdoor location, make sure there are backup options in case of unfavourable weather.

Consider the venue's catering policy as well. Some venues offer in-house catering, while others allow you to bring your own caterers. If you have specific cuisine or dietary preferences, this could be a significant deciding factor.

For a destination wedding, you may want to consider venues that offer lodging or have accommodation options nearby for the convenience of your guests.

Venue Policies:

Lastly, familiarise yourself with the venue's policies. Is there a time restriction for the event? What are their policies on decor and entertainment? Can you bring your vendors, or does the venue require you to work with their preferred vendors? Are there any noise restrictions that could affect your music and entertainment plans?

You should also inquire about their cancellation and rescheduling policies. Given the unpredictability of situations, it's wise to understand these terms before making a commitment.

How to Choose: Conducting Site Visits, Comparing Options, and Negotiating Contracts

After determining your vision and considering factors like location, amenities, and venue policies, you've probably shortlisted a few potential venues. So, how do you make the final choice?

Site Visits:

Visiting the venue in person is an essential step in the selection process. Pictures and descriptions can only convey so much; it's crucial to experience the space firsthand to assess if it aligns with your vision.

When visiting, try to visualise your event in the space. Are there enough areas for different parts of your event like the ceremony, cocktails, and reception? How's the natural lighting, and what would it look like at the time of your event? Does the venue's aesthetic fit your theme or colour scheme?

Ensure to evaluate the facilities like restrooms, changing rooms, kitchen facilities, parking spaces, etc. If possible, visit the venue during an event to see how everything is set up and runs.

Comparing Options:

After you've conducted site visits, it's time to compare your options. List down the pros and cons of each venue and evaluate them against your priority list. Remember, no venue will be perfect, so it's about finding the one that ticks most of your boxes.

Focus more on aspects like the ambiance, available amenities, accessibility for guests, and venue policies.

Negotiating Contracts:

Once you've settled on a venue, it's time to negotiate the contract. Before signing anything, read the contract thoroughly and make sure you understand all the terms and conditions. If there's anything you're not comfortable with or don't understand, don't hesitate to ask for clarification.

If there are specific aspects you're not happy with, don't be afraid to negotiate. Venues often have some flexibility, especially if you're booking in the off-peak season or on a weekday.

Remember to check for any hidden costs, cancellation policies, and what the venue's obligations are in case of unforeseen circumstances like bad weather for outdoor venues.

The Pros and Cons of Various Types of Venues

Traditional Venues: Halls and Hotels

When it comes to weddings, banquet halls and hotels have been the go-to option for quite some time due to their

convenience and grandeur. Now, let's explore the pros and cons of these traditional venues in more detail.

Advantages of Traditional Venues:

1. **Full-Service:** One of the key benefits of choosing a banquet hall or a hotel is that they are often full-service venues. This means they provide all the essentials: tables, chairs, linens, catering, and sometimes even decor and entertainment. The convenience of having everything under one roof can significantly simplify the planning process.

2. **Experienced Staff:** These venues are equipped with experienced staff familiar with hosting weddings, ensuring a smooth operation. They typically have an event coordinator who can guide you through the planning process.

3. **Accommodation:** If you're considering a hotel, another advantage is the availability of rooms for guests. This is particularly beneficial for destination weddings or if many guests are travelling from out of town.

Predictable Weather: With indoor venues like these, you don't need to worry about weather conditions, making them a safe choice year-round.

Disadvantages of Traditional Venues:

1. **Lack of Flexibility:** While the full-service nature of these venues can be a boon, it can also limit flexibility. There may be restrictions on using outside vendors or customising the space to fit your vision.

2. **Less Unique:** As these types of venues are commonly used for weddings, they may lack the uniqueness or personal touch you might desire for your special day.

3. **Availability:** Popular traditional venues book up quickly, especially during peak wedding season. You may need to reserve your date well in advance or be flexible with your wedding date.

4. **Cookie-Cutter Approach:** There's a risk that your event might feel like just another wedding to the venue, leading to a 'cookie-cutter' approach where personalisation may be limited.

Traditional venues are a great choice if you're looking for a hassle-free experience and have a vision that aligns with what the venue offers. However, if you are looking for something more unique or want to personalise every aspect of your wedding, you might need to consider other types of venues.

Destination Weddings: Allure and Challenges

Destination weddings, a concept that has been popularised by numerous celebrity weddings and is increasingly embraced

by couples worldwide, promise a unique and memorable experience. However, alongside the allure, there are certain challenges that come with planning a wedding away from home. Let's dive into both aspects.

The Pros of Destination Weddings:

1. **Unique Experience:** One of the biggest attractions of a destination wedding is the chance to tie the knot in a unique and stunning location. Whether it's a sun-soaked beach, a picturesque vineyard, a historic castle, or a vibrant cityscape, the world is your oyster.

2. **Intimate Celebration:** Destination weddings often lead to smaller guest lists, as not everyone will be able to travel. This results in a more intimate gathering of your closest friends and family, allowing for quality interactions and shared experiences.

3. **Wedding and Honeymoon in One:** With a destination wedding, you can roll your wedding and honeymoon into one. Post-celebration, you can choose to extend your stay and enjoy your honeymoon in the same destination.

4. **Memorable for Guests:** Not only will a destination wedding be a memorable event for you, but it will also be an unforgettable trip for your guests, offering them a mini-vacation and a unique experience.

The Challenges of Destination Weddings:

1. **Logistics and Planning:** Coordinating the logistics of a destination wedding can be challenging. Dealing with vendors remotely, unfamiliarity with local customs or language, and arranging travel and accommodations for guests can all complicate the planning process.

2. **Accessibility and Attendance:** Some of your guests might not be able to travel due to cost, distance, time, or other commitments. This could mean some important people might miss your big day.

3. **Unpredictable Weather:** Depending on the location and time of year, weather can be a factor. Certain destinations might have unpredictable weather patterns that could disrupt outdoor ceremonies or travel plans.

In essence, destination weddings can be a dream come true, offering a unique and intimate celebration in a beautiful location. However, they do come with their set of challenges. Careful planning, potentially with the help of a professional wedding planner experienced in destination weddings, can help you navigate these hurdles and plan an unforgettable wedding.

Unique Venues: Unconventional Charm and Considerations

Apart from traditional and destination wedding venues, a growing trend among couples is to opt for unique, unconventional venues that add an element of surprise and personality to the celebration. These can range from historical sites, museums, art galleries, and botanical gardens to vineyards, barns, or even caves! Each of these unique venues carries its own charm, offering an extraordinary setting for your special day. However, they come with their unique set of pros and cons that need careful consideration.

The Charm of Unique Venues:

1. **Personalised Touch:** Unconventional venues often allow couples to express their personalities, interests, and passions. For instance, history buffs might choose a historical site, wine lovers a vineyard, and nature enthusiasts a botanical garden.

2. **Unique Aesthetic:** These venues typically offer an exceptional aesthetic that can't be replicated in more traditional settings. This unique ambiance can make your wedding stand out and be memorable for you and your guests.

3. **Minimal Decor Needed:** Since these venues come with their inherent charm and character, they often require minimal additional decoration, allowing the natural or historical beauty to shine.

4. **Memorable Experience:** Celebrating in an unconventional venue can provide an exciting and unique experience for your guests, making your wedding truly unforgettable.

Cons for Unique Venues:

1. **Logistics and Limitations:** Unique venues may come with logistical challenges and limitations. For instance, historical sites may have restrictions on noise, light, and decor. Museums and art galleries may require extra precautions to protect their exhibits. Understanding these limitations is crucial when planning your celebration.

2. **Accessibility:** Depending on the location, some unique venues may be less accessible than traditional venues. Considerations around transportation, parking, and accommodation for your guests are important.

3. **Amenities:** Unlike traditional wedding venues, which are equipped to host large events, unique venues might lack certain amenities, such as a commercial kitchen for catering, adequate restroom facilities, or a suitable space for dancing.

4. **Weather Dependency:** If your unique venue is outdoors, like a garden or a vineyard, you might need a backup plan in case of inclement weather.

Choosing a unique, unconventional venue for your wedding can make your celebration distinctly personal and extraordinarily memorable. However, it's essential to thoroughly research and consider the potential challenges associated with your chosen venue. With careful planning and a bit of creativity, these unique spaces can turn your wedding into a one-of-a-kind event.

Home Weddings: Comfort and Complexity

The idea of a home wedding often evokes feelings of intimacy, comfort, and personal charm. Nothing quite beats the sentimental value of getting married in a place that holds many memories, be it your childhood home, a beloved grandparent's house, or even your own home if you've already created one. It offers a chance to celebrate in an environment that is uniquely yours and infuse your day with warmth and personal touches. However, while home weddings can be incredibly beautiful and intimate, they can also present unique challenges that require careful planning and consideration.

The Charm of Home Weddings:

1. **Intimacy:** Home weddings tend to be smaller and more intimate, offering an environment where you can genuinely interact with every guest.

2. **Flexibility:** You have the flexibility to set the wedding schedule and choose the layout that works

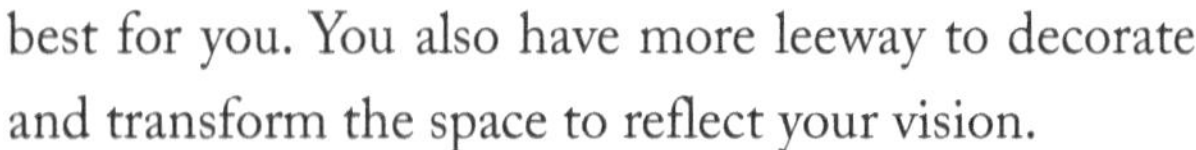

best for you. You also have more leeway to decorate and transform the space to reflect your vision.

3. **Personal Significance:** There's a unique sentimental value associated with getting married in a place tied to your history or daily life. This personal connection can make the celebration even more meaningful.

4. **Cost Considerations:** Depending on the size and scale, home weddings can sometimes be more cost-effective, especially if you're able to cut down on venue rental fees and catering costs.

Challenges of Home Weddings:

1. **Space Constraints:** Depending on the size of your home and property, you may be limited in guest count, and space might be tight for dining, dancing, or even parking.

2. **Rental Requirements:** Most homes aren't equipped to cater to large parties, so you'll likely need to rent essentials like chairs, tables, linens, a dance floor, and possibly even a tent.

3. **Permit and Insurance:** Depending on your location, you might need permits for large gatherings, parking, noise, and more. It's also wise to look into event insurance to protect against damage.

4. **Logistics:** With no venue staff to lean on, you'll be responsible for the setup, clean-up, and coordination

of vendors. Hiring a wedding planner or day-of coordinator can be very helpful in this regard.

5. **Privacy:** Having a large number of guests at your home can also raise issues around privacy and wear and tear on your property.

A home wedding can be a beautiful, memorable celebration. However, planning a wedding at home isn't necessarily an easier or less expensive option than a traditional venue. It requires careful planning, organisation, and an understanding of the responsibilities involved. Still, with the right preparation and support, it can indeed be the intimate, personalised event of your dreams.

WEDDING GUEST LIST

#	GUEST NAME	PHONE NUMBER	ADDRESS/CITY	NUMBER OF GUESTS	CONFIRMED	THANK YOU SENT

Chapter 5

Destination Weddings: The World is Your Stage

In the previous chapter, we navigated the vast and varied landscape of wedding venues, landing at the enchanting shores of destination weddings. Feeling the soft, warm sand beneath our feet, we asked ourselves, "What could be more romantic than exchanging vows in a breathtaking locale that's far from home?" As exotic as it sounds, planning a destination wedding requires a keen eye for detail, a solid understanding of logistics, and, most importantly, a heart yearning for adventure.

In this chapter, we'll help you sort through top-notch wedding destinations, both within the vibrant boundaries of India and some fantastic international hotspots.

Remember, whether it's the serene beaches of Goa, the royal palaces of Rajasthan, the vineyards of Tuscany, or the romantic cobbled streets of Paris, your chosen destination is more than just a backdrop for your wedding. It's an integral part of your love story, setting the stage for the day you say, "I do." So, let's turn the page and start planning your dream wedding in the location of your dreams.

Stunning Indian Destinations

India, with its diverse landscapes and rich cultural heritage, offers a plethora of options for your dream destination wedding. Let's explore some of the top contenders:

Goa: Known as the 'Pearl of the Orient,' Goa is famous for its pristine beaches, Portuguese architecture, and vibrant nightlife. Its laid-back vibes make it a top choice for couples seeking a beachfront wedding.

Kerala: Known as 'God's Own Country,' Kerala's backwaters offer a serene setting for your nuptials. With its lush greenery, tranquil waters, and houseboat ceremonies, it's perfect for a nature-themed wedding.

Andaman Islands: Far from the mainland's bustle, the Andaman Islands are India's best-kept secret for destination weddings. These islands are a treasure trove of sparkling turquoise waters, powdery white sands, and lush tropical forests. Imagine walking down a sandy aisle on Havelock Island, with the Bay of Bengal's gentle waves playing your wedding march. The islands' natural beauty provides a stunning backdrop for both ceremonies and photographs,

ensuring every moment is captured against a canvas of unparalleled allure.

Rajasthan: The land of kings and queens, with its opulent palaces, formidable forts, and sprawling deserts, offers a regal setting for weddings that promises to be nothing short of a fairy tale. The very soil of this state is steeped in stories of valour and romance, making it a coveted destination for couples looking to infuse their wedding with grandeur and historical charm.

In this majestic state, every city adds its unique hue to the palette of wedding destinations.

- **Udaipur:** If you fancy a royal wedding, look no further than Udaipur. Known as the 'City of Lakes,' it boasts majestic palaces, mesmerising lakes, and romantic boat rides.

- **Jaipur:** The 'Pink City' is a haven for those seeking a regal wedding. With its grand palaces, historic forts, and vibrant local culture, Jaipur makes your wedding feel like a royal affair.

- **Jodhpur and Jaisalmer:** These captivating cities of Rajasthan, India, are increasingly popular for destination weddings. Dotted with mighty forts, intricate havelis, and sweeping sand dunes, these royal cities offer a mesmerising backdrop for weddings.

Top International Destinations

For those considering an international destination wedding, there are numerous enchanting locations around the globe. Let's take a look at some favourites.

South East Asia: A Blend of Culture and Natural Beauty

South East Asian countries like Thailand, Malaysia, and Indonesia are renowned for their picturesque landscapes, warm hospitality, and rich cultural heritage, making them ideal for destination weddings.

Sri Lanka:

Sri Lanka beckons couples with its verdant landscapes and golden shores. Tradition and tropical beauty converge to create an unparalleled wedding experience. Whether it's the mystic hills of Kandy, the colonial charm of Galle, or the pristine beaches of the Eastern coast, the island's diverse settings cater to every couple's dream.

The rolling tea gardens and misty hills provide a refreshing escape for highland ceremonies, while the ancient ruins of Anuradhapura and Polonnaruwa offer a majestic plunge into history, perfect for those who wish their union to be surrounded by the grandeur of past civilisations. Along the coast, beachfront resorts in Bentota and Negombo specialise in sun-kissed weddings with the Indian Ocean as a witness.

Maldives:

In the Maldives, love finds a sanctuary amidst the whispers of the sea and the caress of the gentle breeze. It epitomises luxury, intimacy, and scenic beauty, a haven for couples seeking the exclusivity of a private island wedding.

The allure of the Maldives lies not just in its visual splendour but in the meticulous attention to detail provided by the resorts, ensuring a personalised touch to every aspect of the wedding. Here, the horizon stretches endlessly, symbolising the infinite possibilities that the future holds for newlyweds.

Thailand:

Thailand, a land that fuses the mystique of the East with the comforts of the West, offers a myriad of landscapes as varied and vibrant as the traditions thriving within its borders. Known as the Land of Smiles, Thailand's warm hospitality, rich cultural heritage, and breathtaking natural beauty make it a sought after destination for couples looking to tie the knot in an unforgettable locale.

From serene shores to dynamic cityscapes, Thailand presents an array of wedding venues catering to every taste:

- **Hua Hin:** Nestled on the Gulf of Thailand, Hua Hin is known for its stunning beachside resorts and golfing spots. The blend of city and sea makes it an ideal choice for couples who want the best of both worlds.

- **Rayong:** Away from the hustle and bustle of major cities, Rayong boasts tranquil beaches and lush parks. It's a perfect spot for those seeking a quiet, intimate wedding in an unspoilt location.

- **Phuket:** Famous for its blue waters and white sandy beaches, Phuket offers a paradise setting. The island's luxury resorts are known to host spectacular beach weddings amidst the stunning Andaman Sea backdrop.

- **Koh Samui:** This tropical paradise blends luxury with nature. Think breathtaking beachfront ceremonies, candlelit dinners, and celebrations that spill over into the sandy beaches.

- **Bangkok:** The bustling metropolis of Bangkok offers skyscrapers, luxurious hotels, and riverside venues for an urban, chic wedding. A city that never sleeps, it's perfect for couples who want to infuse excitement and energy into their weddings.

Malaysia:

Malaysia is a country where diverse cultures harmonise, where rainforests echo with stories, and where shores whisper tales of the sea. It's a land that offers an eclectic mix of wedding venues, each with its charm, set against the backdrop of Malaysia's rich heritage and natural splendour.

In Malaysia, you can find the perfect spot to exchange vows, whether it's amidst the tranquillity of a tropical beach, within the grandeur of colonial architecture, or against the serenity of a coastal retreat.

- **Langkawi:** Known as the Jewel of Kedah, Langkawi is an archipelago of 99 islands offering white-sand beaches, secluded coves, and luxurious resorts. This tranquil location is ideal for couples who dream of a serene, beachside wedding.

- **Penang:** Celebrated for its historic architecture, cultural sights, and beautiful coastline, Penang offers an intriguing mix for weddings. The city's colonial charm and coastal beauty together create a romantic setting for weddings.

- **Port Dickson:** A coastal town known for its calm beaches and inviting waters. It's a place where time slows down, allowing couples and their guests to bask in the joy of the moment. Resorts in Port Dickson cater to those who wish for a more intimate setting, where the horizon is the altar and the rhythmic waves compose the nuptial music.

Middle Eastern Extravagance:

The Middle East is gaining popularity for its grandeur and luxurious experiences. UAE, with cities like Dubai, Abu Dhabi, Ras Al Khaimah, and Al Ain, offers a blend of modern architecture and traditional Arab culture. A wedding here could be as extravagant as one in a skyscraper

overlooking the city or as intimate as one in a desert camp under the stars.

Other Middle Eastern countries like Bahrain, Qatar, Egypt, and Lebanon also offer unique settings for a wedding, whether it's a beach wedding in Lebanon, a royal wedding in an Egyptian palace, or a modern, chic wedding in Bahrain or Qatar.

UAE

The UAE, with its blend of cityscapes and landscapes, modernity and tradition, sets the scene for weddings of all sizes and styles. The UAE offers a plethora of options for couples looking to step into matrimony with an air of elegance and a touch of Arabian charm.

- **Dubai:** A cosmopolitan oasis with ultra-modern skyscrapers, Dubai offers a luxurious setting for your dream wedding. Here, couples can exchange vows with the stunning backdrop of the Burj Khalifa or amidst the serenity of a lush garden.

- **Abu Dhabi:** Known for its exquisite mosques and waterfront venues, Abu Dhabi provides a blend of tradition and luxury. Couples can choose from beachside resorts, grand ballrooms, or a beautiful garden setting for their weddings.

- **Ras Al Khaimah:** Offering a perfect blend of beachfront resorts and majestic mountains, Ras

Al Khaimah is a hidden gem for a quiet, intimate wedding. The warm desert sands and clear night skies can set the stage for a romantic, starlit ceremony.

Bahrain: Bahrain is a beautiful archipelago known for its pearl fisheries, stunning skyline, and warm hospitality. The city offers a stunning contrast between the modern cityscape and traditional Arabian architecture, making it an eclectic choice for couples.

Qatar: Known for its futuristic skyscrapers and cultural heritage, Qatar offers an interesting mix for a wedding destination. Whether it's a high-end luxury hotel or a traditional Qatari setting, couples can experience a fusion of cultures here.

Lebanon: With its stunning Mediterranean coastline and mountainous landscape, Lebanon offers a diverse range of wedding venues. From beachfront resorts to historical ruins and vineyards, Lebanon provides a picturesque backdrop for any wedding theme.

Muscat: Muscat, Oman's coastal jewel, is a city where tradition meets modern luxury. It's a destination that promises a wedding steeped in Middle Eastern charm without forgoing contemporary comforts. With its pristine beaches, grand mosques, and modern skyline, Muscat offers a unique setting for nuptials.

Turkey

Turkey stands as a testament to the ages, a nation where the whispers of bygone empires meet the pulse of modern life. This cross-continental country offers wedding destinations that mirror its remarkable fusion of diverse cultures and stunning natural backdrops.

- **Antalya:** Antalya, the turquoise coast's shining star, offers a Mediterranean paradise for weddings. It's where the sea meets the sky along expansive beaches, providing a sun-kissed setting for couples to exchange vows. The backdrop of the Taurus Mountains and the blend of beach resorts with historical sites give Antalya a romantic allure unmatched in the Mediterranean.

- **Bodrum:** Bodrum is a city that has charmed seafarers and sun-seekers for millennia. With its whitewashed houses and the Aegean Sea's sapphire waters, it presents a laid-back yet sophisticated atmosphere for nuptials. The city's ancient castle, marinas, and beautiful bays offer a variety of venues that can cater to any preference, from intimate ceremonies to grand, lavish celebrations.

- **Istanbul:** Istanbul is the heart of Turkey and a city where history is alive in every corner. Bridging Asia and Europe, it provides an urban landscape infused with the legacies of empires. From the opulent palaces

like Dolmabahçe and Çırağan to the grandeur of the Hagia Sophia and the Blue Mosque, Istanbul delivers a dramatic and unforgettable wedding experience. The Bosphorus Strait offers a mesmerising venue where couples can celebrate their union with panoramic views of the city's iconic skyline.

European Elegance

Europe, with its rich history, stunning architecture, and diverse cultures, has been a long-time favourite for destination weddings.

Italy:

Italy, a country synonymous with art, culture, and love, is a dream setting for couples seeking a wedding imbued with beauty and timeless elegance. With its romantic landscapes, it promises a wedding right out of a fairytale.

- **Tuscany:** If you dream of a rustic wedding amid vineyards under the Tuscan sun, Tuscany, Italy, is your place. With its picturesque landscapes, historic villas, and delectable cuisine, it offers an unforgettable experience.

- **Lake Como:** Set against the foothills of the Alps, Lake Como offers a dramatic setting for your wedding. With its deep blue waters, lush gardens, and grand villas, a wedding here promises a mix of glamour and old-world romance.

- **Monaco:** Known as a playground for the rich and famous, Monaco offers a glamorous and sophisticated setting for your wedding. Here, couples can choose to get married in a grand palace, a luxury hotel, or even on a yacht overlooking the Mediterranean.

- **Milan:** While Milan is globally renowned as a fashion and design capital, it also offers stunning wedding venues, from grand palaces and gardens to modern, chic spaces. This stylish and vibrant city can serve as an unforgettable backdrop to your special day.

- **Amalfi Coast:** With its cliff-edged azure waters and quaint villages, offers an idyllic setting for weddings. Known for its stunning beauty and romantic atmosphere, it's a perfect spot for couples looking to combine their love with the charm of the Italian seaside. From intimate ceremonies in terraced gardens to celebrations in luxurious villas, a wedding here is an affair to remember.

France

The land, synonymous with romance, offers some of the most exquisite locales for a wedding. Each destination within its borders tells its own love story.

- **Paris:** Known as the 'City of Love,' Paris is a classic choice for a romantic destination wedding. Whether it's an intimate ceremony by the Seine or a grand affair at a historic château, Paris never fails to impress.

- **Cannes:** Nestled along the glittering Côte d'Azur, Cannes is a fusion of star-studded glamour and timeless Mediterranean charm. It's a place where couples can marry amidst the allure of the French Riviera, with its sun-kissed beaches and elegant boulevards. Imagine a ceremony overlooking the azure sea, followed by a reception where the Riviera's famed light dances on the waves.

- **St. Tropez:** A little further along the coast, St. Tropez awaits with its chic, laid-back vibe. This once-sleepy fishing village, which has been transformed into a playground for the artistic and the affluent, offers a picturesque setting for a wedding. The charm of its old port, combined with the beauty of its sandy beaches, provides a relaxed yet sophisticated backdrop perfect for an intimate celebration or a lavish affair.

Greece:

- **Mykonos:** With its iconic windmills and whitewashed buildings, Mykonos sparkles under the Aegean sun. This cosmopolitan island is perfect for couples seeking a lively yet elegant wedding setting. Its beautiful beaches and vibrant nightlife promise a celebration filled with energy and style.

- **Santorini:** The gem of the Cyclades, Santorini is famed for its dramatic views, stunning sunsets, and

volcanic-sand beaches. The island's blue-domed churches and cliff-side venues offer a breathtaking backdrop for an enchanting wedding. It's a place where romance is etched into every sunset and every wave lapping the caldera's edge.

- **Rhodes:** Steeped in history, Rhodes is an island where knights once walked. Its medieval architecture and ancient ruins provide a majestic setting for couples who wish to step back in time on their wedding day. The island's clear waters and beautiful natural landscapes also offer a serene atmosphere for a more traditional beachside ceremony.

Cyprus: Known as the birthplace of Aphrodite, the goddess of love, Cyprus is steeped in mythology and romance. Its sun-drenched beaches, ancient ruins, and fragrant citrus groves create a mystical backdrop for a wedding. Whether you desire a ceremony on a sandy shore or within a rustic vineyard, Cyprus provides a blend of enchantment and tradition for your special day.

Spain: With its vibrant culture, rich history, and diverse landscapes, Spain offers an array of spectacular wedding venues. From the sun-soaked Costa del Sol to the rugged beauty of the Balearic Islands, each location is infused with Spanish passion. Imagine exchanging vows in a medieval castle, a modernist landmark, or amidst the rolling vineyards of the countryside—Spain's charm lies in its variety and the warmth of its people.

Croatia: Croatia's Adriatic coast is a treasure trove of pristine waters, historic cities, and idyllic islands. Dubrovnik's medieval walls and Split's Diocletian's Palace offer a taste of the past, while the Dalmatian Coast's crystal-clear seas provide a tranquil setting. A Croatian wedding combines the allure of the old world with the tranquillity of the Mediterranean.

Montenegro: Montenegro is a rising star in the world of wedding destinations, known for its stunning mountainous landscapes that meet the sea. The Bay of Kotor, with its fortified towns and serene waters, exudes a quiet majesty. For those seeking a blend of natural beauty and Mediterranean charm, Montenegro offers an intimate and unforgettable setting for your wedding.

Africa:

Africa, a continent of boundless skies and diverse landscapes, is home to some of the world's most dramatic and romantic wedding destinations. From its sun-drenched islands to its historic cities, Africa offers an array of breathtaking backdrops for couples looking to celebrate their union.

- **Mauritius:** A jewel in the Indian Ocean, Mauritius is a mosaic of cultures and colours, with azure waters and lush landscapes. It's a tropical paradise where couples can marry on white sandy beaches, in luxurious coastal resorts, or even in the heart of the island's verdant forests. Mauritius combines natural

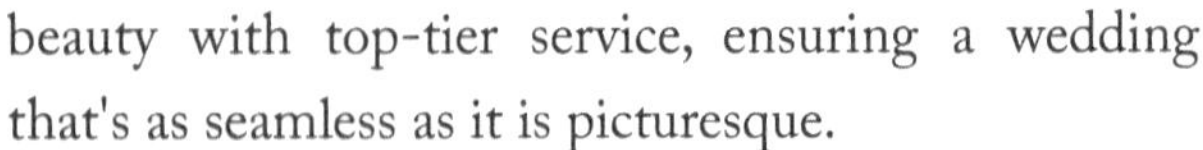

beauty with top-tier service, ensuring a wedding that's as seamless as it is picturesque.

- **Seychelles:** The Seychelles archipelago, with its secluded beaches and rare flora and fauna, is synonymous with exclusivity and tranquillity. The islands serve as a natural sanctuary for a wedding that's private, serene, and intimately connected to the wonders of the natural world. Saying 'I do' on its powdery shores, under the shade of ancient takamaka trees, is nothing short of magical.

- **Morocco:** Morocco is a land where every sunset tells a story, and every landscape is a canvas of contrasts. From the vibrant souks of Marrakech to the majestic Atlas Mountains, Morocco offers a wedding experience infused with rich culture and tradition. Couples can choose from palatial riads, desert oases, or even historic kasbahs for a wedding that beautifully blends Arabic, Berber, and French colonial heritage.

- **Egypt:** Egypt invites couples to make history as they start their future, offering a wedding experience amidst the legacies of pharaohs and the timeless flow of the Nile. Whether it's a luxurious celebration in a Cairo hotel, a romantic cruise on the world's longest river, or even a ceremony with the Great Pyramids as your witnesses, Egypt provides an epic backdrop for your nuptials.

The Other Side of the Atlantic

The Americas and the Caribbean Basin are a patchwork of vibrant cultures, sun-kissed shores, and lush tropical beauty, offering dreamlike settings for weddings that blend adventure with romance.

Hawaii: The Hawaiian Islands are a haven where the aloha spirit enriches every ceremony. With its cascading waterfalls, volcanic landscapes, and beaches in every shade of sand, Hawaii provides a variety of breathtaking backdrops. Couples can exchange leis against the setting sun on a beach in Maui or amidst the lush gardens of Kauai, ensuring a wedding imbued with natural splendour and island charm.

Mexico: From the Mayan Riviera's crystalline waters to the cultural tapestry of Oaxaca, Mexico offers a rich palette of wedding destinations. You can say 'I do' with your toes in the sands of Tulum, within a hacienda's historic walls, or under the vibrant paper flags of a traditional fiesta. Mexican weddings are a colourful celebration of life, love, and joyous beginnings.

Bahamas: The Bahamas, with its archipelago of 700 islands, each with its own personality, offers endless possibilities for nuptial bliss. Whether it's a sophisticated affair at a luxury resort or a barefoot ceremony on a secluded cay, the Bahamas' clear waters and coral gardens promise a wedding that's both serene and spectacular.

Miami: Miami blends the allure of the tropics with the buzz of city life. It's a place where urban chic meets ocean breeze, ideal for couples who crave a contemporary wedding with a touch of beachside tranquillity. Venues range from sleek hotels with rooftop views to sandy shores lined with swaying palms.

The Caribbean: The Caribbean is a symphony of islands, each playing its own melody of romance and beauty. From the old-world elegance of San Juan to the French-infused joie de vivre of St. Barts, the Caribbean islands offer settings so idyllic they seem to leap from the pages of a storybook. Here, weddings are as diverse as the islands themselves, characterised by clear skies, warm waters, and an unwavering spirit of celebration.

Logistics and Cultural Considerations

Let's talk logistics, shall we? When it comes to destination weddings, the devil is indeed in the details. It's a bit more than just picking out a beautiful location; it's about making sure everything runs smoothly when you and your guests get there.

You're going to have to think about accommodation and transport. Now, don't start pulling your hair out yet! You don't have to do it all alone. This is where a seasoned wedding planner who knows the ropes of destination weddings can save the day. They've got contacts, they know the area, and

they're experts at making things happen just the way you want it.

And yes, transportation. You're not just thinking about how everyone's going to get there but also how they'll get around once they're there. Will your guests have to rent cars, or can they walk to the venues? Is there a shuttle service available? Making sure everyone can get to where they need to be comfortably is a key part of the planning process.

Embracing Local Culture:

This is where it gets really exciting! You've picked a destination; now it's time to dive into its unique culture. If you're tying the knot in a country that's different from your own, get to know the customs and traditions. You don't have to include everything in your wedding, but a little local flavour can definitely make your celebration stand out.

Weather is another thing that's tied to your chosen location. If you're jetting off to a beach, think light and breezy when it comes to what you'll wear. Heading somewhere that might have a sudden downpour? Have a plan B in place. You don't want your dream day to turn into a 'singing in the rain' moment – unless that's your thing, of course!

Now, food! Who doesn't love trying out local cuisine? It's a wonderful way to give your guests a real taste of the culture.

Just remember, everyone has different tastes and dietary needs, so a variety of options is a must.

Planning a Seamless Destination Wedding Experience

Now that we've gotten a grasp on the logistics and cultural considerations, let's delve into the real deal: how to plan a seamless destination wedding experience.

Picking the Right Team:

Okay, let's be honest. No matter how much of a superhuman you think you are, planning a destination wedding is not a one-person job. You're going to need a team that has your back.

A great wedding planner who has a handle on destination weddings can be a real game-changer. They'll help you navigate the whole process and take a load off your shoulders.

Consider other key players like caterers, photographers, videographers, and decorators who are familiar with your chosen location. Their local knowledge can often prove invaluable. And let's not forget about a stellar makeup artist and hairstylist to ensure you look your best on your special day!

Clear Communication:

Miscommunication can lead to mishaps, and we want to avoid that, right? Ensure clear communication with your guests. Inform them about the itinerary, transport, accommodations, dress codes, or any other significant

details. You could create a wedding website or a group chat to keep everyone in the loop.

Plan Activities:

When you host a destination wedding, you're essentially inviting your loved ones on a mini-vacation. So why not make it as fun-filled as possible? Plan activities like local sightseeing tours, a welcome party, or a post-wedding brunch. These extra touches will make your wedding a memorable affair for everyone involved.

Mindful Planning:

Remember, it's not just about the wedding day but also the days leading up to it. The travel, time zones, and possible jet lag can take a toll on you and your guests. So, plan some downtime. Let everyone relax, rejuvenate, and be ready to celebrate.

You see, planning a destination wedding isn't just about saying 'I do' in a stunning location. It's about crafting an experience that's memorable, not just for you but for your guests as well. But hey, don't sweat the small stuff too much – it's going to be one heck of an adventure!

Chapter 6

Picture Perfect: Capturing the Moments

I t's been a decade since your wedding. You're sitting on a comfy couch with your loved one, flipping through your wedding album or scrolling through digital images. The memories come flooding back, making you laugh, making you nostalgic, and yes, making you fall in love all over again. That's the magic of captured moments!

Your wedding day will fly by faster than you could ever imagine. Between greeting guests, enjoying the ceremonies, and dancing the night away, you'll be surprised how quickly it all passes. Capturing these fleeting moments in photos or videos ensures that you can relive this special day whenever you want.

Not just for you, but these captured memories will also serve as a testament of love for future generations. Imagine the joy of your grandchildren as they see you, decades younger, on one of the happiest days of your life. They might laugh at the fashion of our time, but the emotions captured will undoubtedly touch their hearts.

So, wedding photography and videography isn't merely about taking pictures or shooting videos; it's about encapsulating emotions, laughter, tears, rituals, and everything in between.

Understanding Wedding Photography

Photographs are time machines, right? They freeze moments for us to revisit later. But here's the thing: not all moments are captured in the same way. So, let's do a quick crash course on the different styles and approaches to wedding photography.

- **Traditional Photography:** Think posed photos with everyone looking at the camera. These are your 'safe shots' – the ones with your family, bridal party, and, of course, the bride and groom. This style ensures that everyone important is photographed, but it might miss some candid, raw emotions.

- **Photojournalistic:** Here, the photographer tells your wedding story through a candid, narrative approach. It's less about posed photos and more about spontaneous, in-the-moment shots. You might find the photographer blending into the background to capture real, raw emotions.

- **Fine Art:** This style gives the photographer artistic licence to inject their point of view into the photographs. You'll see unique angles, focus on details, and a lot of attention on aesthetics and composition. Your wedding photos could end up looking like pieces of art!

- **Fashion/Editorial:** This is all about dramatic compositions and poses, glamorous style, and high-end finish. Think glossy magazines, and you're on the right track. If you love the glitz and glam, this might be your style.

Remember, most photographers don't stick strictly to one style. They blend and switch between different styles to capture your wedding in its entirety. The key is to understand these styles and communicate your preferences with your chosen photographer. So, are you ready for your close-up?

These are just a few styles to start with. There's also black and white photography, vintage photography, and so much more.

Understanding Wedding Videography

Alright, so we've unravelled the mystery of photography styles, but let's not forget the moving pictures – yes, I'm talking about videos. If photographs are time machines, then videos are the magic carpets that carry you back in time to relive the moments, emotions, and even the music of your special day. So, let's dive into the enchanting world of wedding videography!

- **Cinematic Style:** Like a movie director, a videographer using the cinematic style will narrate your love story with some Hollywood flair. This style is characterised by a high-quality film-like look with special attention to lighting, angles, and sophisticated editing techniques. It's all about drama, glamour, and creating an emotionally charged wedding film.

- **Documentary Style:** If you want a no-frills, honest capture of your wedding day, then this is your style. Here, the videographer acts as a fly on the wall, documenting the day as it unfolds without influencing or directing the events. The final result is a chronological, candid capture of your special day.

- **Music Video Style:** Want your wedding video to rock and roll? Then the Music Video style might be your jam! This style often features one or more music tracks over which various wedding scenes are edited. It's fun, it's upbeat, and it's definitely not your traditional wedding video.

- **Short-Form Wedding Film:** If you like the idea of a 'highlights reel', then the short-form style might be for you. These are usually less than 30 minutes and capture the essence of your wedding day, focusing on the most impactful moments and emotions.

- **Drone Videography:** Want to add a bird's eye view of your beautiful wedding venue? Drone videography can provide awe-inspiring aerial shots, adding a new perspective and grandeur to your wedding video.

Just like photography, videography styles can also be mixed and matched. It's essential to pick a videographer whose style resonates with your vision.

Creating a Wedding Album That Tells Your Story

Setting the narrative for your wedding album isn't just about selecting your favourite photos and sticking them onto beautiful pages. It's much more akin to creating a storybook – a storybook that's filled to the brim with love, laughter, tears, and moments that take you right back to your big day. So, let's get down to the nuts and bolts of how you can create a cohesive narrative with your wedding photos and videos.

First things first – the chronological order. A sequential arrangement of your photos and videos will make your wedding story flow naturally. Start with the pre-wedding shoots or behind-the-scenes pictures of the wedding preparations. Then, move on to the main ceremony, ensuring you include the key moments – the walk down the aisle, the vows, the ring exchange, and the first kiss. Don't forget to capture the smiles, the tears, and the joy in the crowd. And, of course, wrap it up with the grand exit or the reception party madness!

But a true narrative goes beyond a mere timeline. It's about the emotions and small, magical moments that bind the day together. Candid shots are perfect for this. That look of anticipation as you wait for your partner at the altar, the tear glistening in your father's eye, the hearty laughter at the best man's speech, the kids sneaking in an extra piece of cake – these are the raw, real moments that bring your wedding story to life.

Then, there's the element of themes and motifs. Do you have a colour scheme, a special symbol, or a recurring theme at your wedding? Incorporating these elements into your album design will make your story more cohesive and visually harmonious.

Finally, don't forget to include your voices in the album. Anecdotes, vows, speeches, or even short love notes to each other can be incorporated into the design. These words will add depth and a personal touch to your narrative, making it truly your own.

Selecting the Right Photographer and Videographer:

Finding the right professionals to document your wedding is crucial. After all, they are the ones who will capture the fleeting moments and nuanced emotions of your big day. Here's a rundown on how to select the right photographer

and videographer who can accurately translate your vision into stunning photos and films.

- **Style Sensibility:** Every photographer and videographer has a unique style, be it traditional, photojournalistic, editorial, or artistic. Browse through their portfolios and social media channels. Do you like their use of light, angles, and composition? Does their style resonate with you?

- **Personality Match:** Your photographer and videographer will be with you throughout your wedding day, so it's important to feel comfortable around them. Schedule a meet-up or a video call to gauge their personality. Do they put you at ease? Are they receptive to your ideas?

- **Experience and Expertise:** How experienced are they in shooting weddings? Are they familiar with your venue or the kind of ceremony you're planning? An experienced professional can anticipate moments, work under pressure, and handle unexpected situations gracefully.

- **Check References:** Look for reviews and testimonials from past clients. This can provide insights into their work ethic, punctuality, and professionalism.

- **Understand Their Process:** Discuss their working style. How do they plan and coordinate? Do they have any backup plans in case of unforeseen circumstances? How soon can they deliver the

final product? Clarity in these areas can prevent misunderstandings down the line.

- **Share Your Story:** Give them a good understanding of your love story, your wedding theme, and the specific moments or details you want captured. The more they know, the better they can reflect your story in their work.

So, take your time to find professionals who understand and appreciate your vision. Don't forget to express your personal preference – after all, you are the star of the show!

Chapter 7

Entertainment Unplugged

Ready to dive into the rhythm of the big day? I bet you are! You've got the perfect venue and the most stunning attire, but let's not forget one thing that keeps the spirits high and the feet tapping – the Entertainment! Oh yes, from that high-energy Sangeet to the grandeur of the reception, every event calls for its own brand of amusement and enjoyment.

In this chapter, we're all set to unleash the Entertainment Quotient. We're talking DJs spinning the decks, live bands crooning your favourite tunes, and performing artists adding that pinch of drama and heaps of fun. Plus, we've got some innovative and engaging entertainment ideas up our sleeves. So let's crank up the volume and set the stage because when it comes to a wedding, it's showtime, folks! And trust me, with the right entertainment, you'll have your guests reminiscing about your wedding for years to come!

Let's start with a simple truth – weddings are celebrations, and what's a celebration without some form of entertainment? The importance of entertainment at a wedding can't be understated. It breathes life into the ceremony, keeping your guests engaged and amused throughout the different stages of the event. More than that, it sets the tone and the mood for your big day. Whether it's an upbeat Sangeet that gets everyone grooving or a sentimental reception where you have your first dance as a married couple, entertainment is the magic wand that transforms your wedding into an unforgettable experience.

However, entertainment is more than just having a DJ or a live band playing in the background. It's about creating moments, spreading joy, and even representing the couple's personality or love story. Your chosen entertainment can be the icebreaker for guests who may not know each other, serving as a catalyst for laughter and conversation. It can be the vehicle that carries your guests through the emotional journey of your love story, culminating in the climax of your union.

Furthermore, the entertainment you select can also serve as a reflection of your culture, traditions, and personal taste. It's a unique opportunity to show your guests who you are as a couple while also thanking them for being a part of your special day. From a traditional folk dance performance

to an avant-garde fire dancer spectacle, the entertainment at your wedding can be as unique and memorable as you want it to be!

In essence, the entertainment you choose plays a critical role in shaping the experience and memories of your wedding, both for you and your guests. So, let's dive in and discover how to make your big day the most entertaining event of the year!

Exploring Entertainment Options

We have an entire orchestra of entertainment options to choose from for our weddings these days, each with its unique flair. While the choice often depends on personal preference, cultural background, and the wedding's overall theme, let's have a quick tour of some of the most popular options.

Starting with DJs, they're like the life of the party, aren't they? With their electrifying energy, they can light up the dance floor and get everyone grooving to their beats, making them a great choice for Sangeet or the reception night. They're versatile, catering to diverse music preferences, and often come with their lighting effects and dance floor setups. Plus, a DJ's charisma can also set the right mood and keep the party going all night long.

On the other hand, if you're looking for a more sophisticated and classy vibe, hiring a live band could be the perfect

choice. Bands can perform a wide range of music genres and can offer a more personalised and intimate entertainment experience. Plus, there's something magical about live music, isn't there? It adds a certain depth and richness to the ambiance that recorded music often can't match.

The entertainment you choose for your wedding is an extension of your celebration. It's about creating an atmosphere of joy, warmth, and festivity that resonates with your vision of the perfect wedding day. So, take your time to explore, choose what aligns with your personality and theme, and let's set the stage on fire!

The Live Band: Creating a Magical Atmosphere

From stirring emotions with romantic ballads to making guests groove to peppy numbers, a live band can bring a unique charm to your wedding festivities. There's something undeniably captivating about live music that a recorded playlist often can't replicate. If you're thinking about hiring a live band, let's discuss their role, what they're responsible for, and some tips to keep in mind during the hiring process.

A live band at a wedding is like adding a dash of magic to your celebration. They can perform a range of musical genres to cater to different moods of the event, from soft background music during the cocktail hour to energetic performances to kick off the dance party. Many bands also

take song requests from guests, making the experience more interactive and personalised.

In terms of responsibilities, live bands usually provide their own musical instruments, sound equipment, and often lighting, making it easier for you. They might also coordinate with the venue regarding setup and logistics, ensuring a seamless performance.

Hiring a live band requires some homework, though. It's essential to see them perform live, if possible, before you book them. This gives you a better understanding of their energy, stage presence, and how they interact with the crowd. Discuss with them your wedding's theme and desired atmosphere, as well as any specific songs or genres you'd like them to include or avoid. Also, ensure that they are comfortable performing the first dance song if you have one in mind.

Don't forget to read reviews, ask for references, and ensure they have experience performing at weddings. Each event has a different energy and flow, and you want a band that can handle the dynamics of a wedding.

Interactive Entertainment: Engage, Participate and Revel

The most memorable weddings are the ones that get the guests off their chairs and onto the dance floor. Interactive entertainment is a wonderful way to ensure your guests are not merely spectators but active participants in your

celebration. In this section, we delve into some of the most engaging and participatory entertainment options that are sure to make your wedding a hit.

When we think about a wedding, we often envision a vibrant atmosphere full of energy, laughter, and lots and lots of dancing. And that's precisely what a DJ brings to a wedding. Let's dive a little deeper into their role, responsibilities, and a few points to ponder when hiring one for your big day.

Firstly, a DJ does much more than just play a list of songs. They are the heart and soul of your celebration, setting the mood and keeping your guests entertained throughout. A good DJ can read the crowd, adjusting their music to keep the dance floor lively and the energy levels high. They play a mix of slow and fast songs, old and new, catering to the diverse age groups and musical tastes at a wedding. In essence, they ensure there's something for everyone.

As for responsibilities, apart from playing music, a DJ may also provide sound equipment and lighting setups and even serve as the emcee, making announcements and ensuring the event's smooth flow.

Now, when it comes to hiring a DJ, there are a few things to consider. You'll want to ensure they have a comprehensive understanding of the wedding's theme and vibe. It's also crucial to discuss the song preferences, any 'do not play'

songs, and special requests beforehand. Make sure to check their experience, especially with weddings, as managing a wedding crowd is a skill in itself. Finally, don't forget to read reviews and ask for references from past clients. After all, you want to ensure the person responsible for the entertainment shares your vision of a fantastic wedding party.

One of the most popular interactive entertainment ideas is the classic dance-off. Dance-offs not only get your guests moving and shaking but also instil a sense of friendly competition that elevates the fun. Whether it's the bridesmaids versus groomsmen or a face-off between different families, dance-offs can be customised to suit your wedding's theme and atmosphere.

Karaoke is another fantastic way to get your guests involved. With a microphone in hand and a selection of everyone's favourite tunes, karaoke can bring even the shyest guests to centre stage. Imagine your aunt belting out a classic or your best friend crooning to a romantic song; these are the moments that make your wedding truly unforgettable.

Interactive entertainment isn't just about getting on stage. You can also think about adding interactive installations, like photo booths with props and costumes or an interactive guest book where guests can leave a video message. These elements keep your guests engaged throughout the event and give them something fun to do between the main events.

Let's remember that entertainment at your wedding is about creating an atmosphere of joy and celebration. The goal is to offer your guests an experience that resonates with them long after the event. We aren't just crafting a wedding but a celebration that is as unforgettable as your love story!

Chapter 8

Dress to Impress!

Stepping into the spotlight, all eyes on you, heart fluttering with excitement, you want to make sure you look your absolute best on your big day. Your attire, a splendid symbol of celebration, plays a leading role in this grand performance. This chapter, dear readers, is all about the fascinating world of wedding wardrobes, a dazzling domain where style meets tradition. As we tread the path from exquisitely crafted designer ensembles to creative DIY solutions, we'll also delve into the intricate nuances of wedding attire etiquette. Buckle up for a fashion-forward journey as we help you navigate the myriad choices so you can truly 'dress to impress' at your wedding!

Decoding the Indian Wedding Wardrobe: A Primer on Attire for Different Ceremonies

Indian weddings are not a one-day affair. They are elaborate multi-day celebrations, each day featuring a different ceremony with its unique dress code. Here, we'll walk you through the various festivities and their corresponding attire, setting the stage for your sartorial journey.

To start, let's discuss the Haldi ceremony, where bright and vibrant shades of yellow or gold are the norm. These colours symbolise purity, prosperity, and happiness. For the Mehendi, women often opt for lighter fabrics like georgette or chiffon in cheerful hues, allowing for easy movement while their henna is applied. Men usually sport comfortable kurtas in complementary colours.

Then comes the Sangeet, a lively musical night that calls for something glitzy and glamorous. Rich fabrics, ornate embroidery, sparkling sequins, and vibrant colours are popular choices for both men and women. Ladies often go for lehengas or anarkalis, while men may opt for sherwanis or Indo-western suits.

For the main wedding ceremony, traditional attire takes centre stage. Women usually wear heavily embroidered lehengas, sarees, or salwar suits in red or pink shades, while men don elaborate sherwanis or dhotis in regal tones.

Finally, for the reception, gowns and tuxedos are common among modern couples, though traditional Indian attire is still a popular choice. The key here is to choose something that exudes elegance and sophistication.

Bridal Wear: Exploring the Styles, Trends, and Traditions

The Indian bridal ensemble is a striking showcase of tradition, intricacy, and elegance, often replete with rich fabrics and exquisite detailing. Each piece, from the main garment to the myriad of accessories, plays a crucial role in creating the perfect bridal look.

Lehengas, for instance, are a perennial favourite among Indian brides. These voluminous skirts paired with a cropped blouse and a flowing dupatta come in a plethora of styles, colours, and fabrics. Traditional red lehengas, symbolising fertility and prosperity, are a classic choice, but modern brides are increasingly experimenting with other hues, like peach, pink, and even blues and greens.

Sarees are another popular option, with their style and fabric often varying significantly by region. From the bright red and gold Benarasi silk sarees of the north to the white and gold Kasavu sarees of Kerala in the south, each tells a story of local artistry and heritage.

Salwar suits, particularly the heavily embroidered Anarkalis or Shararas, also make stunning bridal outfits, especially for pre-wedding ceremonies like Mehendi or Sangeet.

Trends in bridal wear also extend to embellishments and detailing. Traditional embroidery techniques like zari, zardozi, gota patti, and kundan add a regal touch to bridal

outfits, while crystal or sequin work provides a modern sparkle.

Accessories, too, form an integral part of the bridal look. Statement jewellery, intricately designed 'mehendi,' and ornate 'bindis' and 'bangles' enhance the overall aesthetic of the bride.

Whether you choose to go the traditional route or mix in contemporary elements, the goal is to feel comfortable and radiate confidence.

Groom's Attire: Embracing Tradition and Modernity

While often outshone by the bride's ensemble, the groom's attire is no less significant. Like bridal wear, the groom's clothing in Indian weddings is steeped in cultural symbolism and varies greatly depending on the region and community.

The traditional sherwani remains a popular choice among grooms. This long, coat-like garment, usually made of heavier fabrics like silk or brocade and adorned with intricate embroidery or handwork, exudes a royal charm. Pairing a sherwani with a contrasting 'dupatta' or 'sehra' – a traditional groom's headgear – creates a striking look.

For a more relaxed but equally stylish choice, many grooms opt for Kurta-Pyjama sets. A 'Pathani' suit, with

its characteristic cuffed pants and loose kurta, offers a chic, contemporary spin on this classic look.

'Achkans' and 'Bandhgalas', popular in North India, are also making a comeback. These button-up coats, often paired with 'Jodhpuri' pants, deliver an elegant, tailored look.

In Southern India, grooms often wear 'Dhotis' or 'Vestis', wide lengths of fabric skillfully wrapped around the waist. These are typically worn with a kurta or an 'Angavastram', a piece of cloth draped over the shoulders.

In terms of colours, while cream, gold, and other earthy tones continue to be the norm, grooms are gradually breaking away from tradition and experimenting with bolder colours like blues, purples, and even pinks.

The choice of footwear, often 'Mojaris' or 'Juttis' – traditional Indian handcrafted leather shoes – and accessories like 'Kalgi', 'Mala', and 'Kamarband' further accentuate the groom's attire.

Whether you're a groom favouring classic styles or looking to make a fashion-forward statement, it's crucial to choose attire that reflects your personality while ensuring you're comfortable throughout the festivities.

Sourcing Outfits – From Designer to DIY

Navigating the world of wedding fashion can seem daunting, given the sheer number of options available. However,

finding that perfect ensemble boils down to your personal style, comfort, and budget. Whether you wish to don a bespoke creation from a renowned designer or add personal touches through DIY, we'll help you explore the various routes to creating your dream wedding wardrobe.

Designer Outfits: The Craftsmanship of Elegance and Style

For those seeking a distinctive, high-quality ensemble for their special day, designer outfits are a go-to option. The appeal of designer outfits lies in their exclusivity, intricate detailing, and superior craftsmanship. Each garment is often a work of art, reflecting the designer's unique aesthetic.

Working with a designer involves an exciting journey of discovery. It often starts with an initial consultation to discuss your vision, theme, preferred colours, and silhouette. The designer then presents sketches or mood boards based on your input. Once a design is finalised, detailed measurements are taken to ensure a perfect fit. Multiple fittings and reviews might follow to fine-tune the outfit.

You can choose to go ahead with well-reputed designers and their creations admired for their fusion of traditional techniques with contemporary designs. Alternatively, emerging designers offer fresh perspectives and might align well with your style at possibly more accessible price points.

Pros and Cons of Designer Outfits

Pros:

1. **Unique and Customised:** Designer outfits are often bespoke creations tailored to your preferences, ensuring your outfit is as unique as you are. It's a chance to wear something that truly represents your personal style.

2. **High-Quality Materials:** Designers use top-notch fabric, embellishments, and materials, which contribute to the outfit's overall look, feel, and longevity.

3. **Professional Guidance:** Designers provide professional advice on what works best for your body type, skin tone, and wedding theme, ensuring you look your absolute best.

4. **Attention to Detail:** Designer outfits are known for their exquisite attention to detail. From the precision of the fit to the intricacy of the embellishments, every aspect is meticulously crafted.

Cons:

1. **Time-Consuming:** The process of creating a designer outfit involves multiple consultations, fittings, and revisions, which can be time-consuming.

2. **Limited Flexibility:** While you get a say in the design process, the final design decisions often lie with the

designer. You may need to compromise on some of your ideas.

3. **Duplication Risk:** Despite the exclusivity of designer wear, popular designs can be replicated in the market. This can detract from the uniqueness of your outfit.

Ready-to-Wear: For the Busy Bees

Ready-to-wear wedding attire is an excellent alternative for those who have limited time or simply prefer the convenience of choosing an outfit off-the-rack. Let's explore this option more closely.

Top Brands: India boasts an array of brands that offer high-quality ready-to-wear wedding outfits. These brands offer a wide selection of designs, colours, and fabrics that cater to diverse tastes. They have outfits that echo tradition and also experiment with modern aesthetics.

International brands, on the other hand, offer Western-style wedding outfits. They often feature a dedicated wedding collection with contemporary silhouettes and designs.

Shopping Tips: When buying ready-to-wear wedding attire, consider these tips:

- **Know Your Size:** Understanding your measurements is key to finding an outfit that fits well. Most brands provide a size chart, so use that as a guide.

- **Plan Ahead:** While you don't need as much lead time as with designer wear, it's good to start shopping a few weeks in advance to account for any alterations that might be needed.

- **Inspect Thoroughly:** Make sure to inspect the outfit thoroughly for any defects before purchasing. Check the seams, embroidery, and any embellishments.

- **Try Before You Buy:** If possible, try on the outfit before making the purchase. This will give you a sense of how it looks on you and how comfortable you feel in it.

- **Accessories Matter:** Keep in mind the accessories you plan to wear with the outfit. They should complement the outfit and not overshadow it.

Pros and Cons of DIY Wedding Outfits

Pros:

- **Personal Touch:** A DIY wedding outfit will be unique, with elements that speak directly to your personality, style, and the love story you're celebrating.

- **Cost-Effective:** Depending on the materials used, DIY can often be a more cost-effective way to create a stunning outfit that won't break the bank.

- **Creative Expression:** If you're a creative person, designing and creating your own wedding outfit can be an incredibly fulfilling project.

Cons:

- **Time-Consuming:** Making your own wedding outfit can be a lengthy process, requiring a substantial investment of time. Between the design, sourcing materials, and the actual creation, it can be quite intensive.

- **Skills Needed:** Unless you're skilled at sewing or have a strong understanding of garment construction, creating a wedding outfit could be challenging.

- **Potential Stress:** Weddings are often high-stress times, and if things don't go to plan with your DIY project, it can add to the stress levels.

The Timeless Tradition of Heirloom Wedding Outfits

Amidst the bustling marketplaces and renowned designers' studios, there's a treasure trove of wedding attire that often remains overshadowed: the heirloom wedding outfits. These aren't just pieces of clothing; they are intricately woven memories, stories of love, tales of commitment, and legacies passed down through generations.

When a bride or groom dons an heirloom outfit, they're not just wearing a piece of clothing; they're wearing history. They're enveloped in the love of the generations that came before them. Every delicate thread and bead tells a story, echoing with the laughter and tears of yesteryears, carrying the blessings and hopes of ancestors.

Take, for instance, the saree passed down from a grandmother to her granddaughter. It's not just about the fabric or the design; it's about the day the grandmother wore it, the way she felt, the promises she made, and the life she built thereafter. When the granddaughter wraps that very saree around her, she's enveloped in a tapestry of stories, dreams, and memories that transcend time.

Men, too, inherit the legacy. The sherwani that a grandfather wore, with its intricate embroidery and traditional motifs, can be carefully preserved and handed down to his grandson. It stands as a testament to the heritage, culture, and familial bonds that have remained strong through the test of time.

Moreover, modern couples are often infusing contemporary touches into these heirlooms, ensuring they reflect both their personal style and deep-rooted traditions. They might update certain elements, add new accessories, or blend the old with the new to create a unique ensemble that pays homage to the past while looking toward the future.

Opting for an heirloom outfit is also a beautiful way to honour and remember loved ones who may no longer be with us. It's a symbolic way to ensure that they, too, are a part of this joyous occasion, watching over and showering their blessings.

And there you have it – a comprehensive look at the world of wedding attire, from traditions to trends and everything in between. No matter the route you choose, remember your wedding outfit should be a reflection of you. It's not merely about following fashion or pleasing the crowd. Your wedding day is one where you should feel comfortable, beautiful, and true to yourself. So, whether you opt for a designer masterpiece, an off-the-rack gem, or a DIY marvel, the goal is to find an outfit that matches your vision for this special day. After all, when you're dressed to impress, it adds an extra layer of magic to your wedding experience.

Chapter 9

Food for the Soul

FOOD! The universal language of love, comfort, and celebration. When it comes to an Indian wedding, the feast is often what people remember long after the couple has said their vows. Yes, the decor might be sparkling, and the music might be foot-tapping, but it's the spread of sumptuous dishes that gets the tongues wagging. In this tantalising chapter, we're diving deep into the art of crafting a drool-worthy menu that resonates with the soul. Buckle up, food lovers; it's going to be a scrumptious ride!

Setting the Tone: Understanding Your Guests' Preferences

Planning a wedding menu isn't just about choosing your favourite dishes; it's a culinary symphony where each note must harmonise with your guests' tastes and preferences. After all, what's a feast if it doesn't feed the soul?

- **Know Your Audience:** Begin by understanding the profile of your guests. Is it a younger crowd craving modern twists or an older gathering who loves traditional flavours? Maybe a mix of both? Tailoring your menu to please the majority sets a harmonious tone right from the start.

- **Consider Cultural Sensitivities:** Indian weddings can be a melting pot of diverse cultures and traditions. Ensure that your menu respects and celebrates these differences. For instance, you may want to avoid beef in a predominantly Hindu gathering or pork in a Muslim crowd.

- **Surveys and Invitations:** A clever way to gauge preferences is by including a section on dietary preferences in the wedding invitation or conducting a quick survey among close family and friends. It's like asking, "Hey, what would you love to eat at our wedding?" and it adds a personal touch to your planning.

- **Incorporate a Variety:** Aim for a balanced menu that caters to different tastes and dietary needs. Include vegetarian and non-vegetarian options, spice levels, and dishes that cater to both traditional and contemporary tastes.

- **Think Seasonally:** Aligning the menu with the season not only ensures fresh and flavoursome ingredients but can also connect with regional specialities that resonate with the locale of the wedding.

Choosing the right type of service for your wedding meal isn't just about aesthetics; it's about creating an atmosphere that complements the theme and vibe of your big day. Here's a look at the two most popular styles, Buffet and Plated Service, along with their unique characteristics.

Menu Types: Buffet vs. Plated Service

Buffet Service

Pros:

- **Variety:** With a buffet, the world (or the kitchen) is your oyster. Guests can pick and choose from a wide array of dishes, ensuring everyone finds something they love.

- **Casual Atmosphere:** Buffets promote a relaxed environment where guests can mingle, chat, and create their own perfect plate.

- **Flexibility:** Buffets can cater to dietary restrictions more easily, as guests control what ends up on their plates.

Cons:

- **Potential for Waste:** If not managed well, a buffet can lead to overserving and wasted food.

- **Lines and Waiting:** No one likes to wait in line, especially when they're hungry. Buffets can create queues and a bit of chaos if not handled efficiently.

Plated Service

Pros:

- **Elegance:** There's something inherently sophisticated about a beautifully plated meal served directly to your guests.
- **Controlled Portions:** Plated service means controlled serving sizes, helping to minimise waste.
- **Smooth Flow:** Guests remain seated, allowing for a more structured flow to the event, which may align better with formal or traditional weddings.

Cons:

- **Limited Choices:** Plated meals often mean limited options. While you can offer choices in advance, it doesn't provide the same breadth of variety as a buffet.
- **Complex Logistics:** Managing individual preferences and dietary restrictions, and ensuring timely service, requires meticulous planning and coordination.
- **Hybrid Approach:** Some couples opt for a blend of both, such as a plated main course with buffet-style appetisers or desserts. This combines the elegance of plated service with the variety and flexibility of a buffet.

Catering to Diverse Palates: More Than Just a Menu

Let's take a journey through a global culinary landscape where tastes, textures, and traditions intertwine to create an extraordinary wedding feast. In this kaleidoscope of flavours, catering to diverse palates isn't just about satisfying hunger—it's an expression of inclusivity, care, and respect for your guests' unique preferences and dietary choices. After all, what's more heartwarming than a meal crafted with love and awareness? One such consideration that is growing in importance is offering vegetarian and vegan options. Let's dig into this plant-based paradise.

Fusion Cuisine: Blending Traditions

In an increasingly globalised world, fusion cuisine has emerged as a trendy and exciting culinary choice, especially at multifaceted events like weddings. Fusion cuisine is all about combining elements of different culinary traditions and presenting them in a cohesive, innovative way. This often means blending flavours, techniques, and ingredients from various cultures.

A fusion menu at a wedding can reflect the personal tastes of the couple, celebrating their unique cultural backgrounds, or simply catering to a more adventurous audience. Imagine dishes that pair traditional Indian spices with European

cooking techniques, or Asian-inspired salads served alongside classic Indian curries.

However, this blending of traditions is not without its challenges. The balance must be right, and the fusion should not become a confusion. It requires a skilled chef who understands both the cuisines being fused, respecting their individual characteristics while creating something novel and harmonious. Choosing fusion cuisine adds an avant-garde twist to the wedding feast, making it a memorable culinary experience for guests seeking something out of the ordinary.

Children's Menu: Pleasing the Little Ones

Don't forget about the youngest guests! Catering to children at a wedding may seem like a small detail, but it can make a significant difference in how enjoyable the event is for families. Children's palates are usually different from adults', and a menu tailored to their tastes can keep them happy and engaged.

Consider including familiar and beloved kids' favourites like mini pizzas, chicken nuggets, mac and cheese, or fruit skewers. Adding creative twists to these classics can also make them more appealing to the little ones. For example, a pasta dish in fun shapes or sliders that are just the right size for small hands.

Offering a children's menu is more than just a thoughtful gesture; it ensures that parents can relax and enjoy the event, knowing that their children are content with their meals. It can also be an opportunity to introduce children to new flavours and foods in a friendly, non-threatening way.

The Revival of Traditional Indian Wedding Dishes

In the fast-paced world of wedding planning, trends come and go, but there's something timeless about honouring the roots and traditions that make a culture rich and vibrant. The revival of traditional Indian wedding dishes is a nod to this cultural richness, giving new generations a taste of history and heritage. Let's explore some facets of this exciting culinary journey:

Rediscovering Lost Recipes

Over time, many traditional Indian recipes have faded from common use and been replaced by more contemporary dishes. However, there's a growing movement towards reviving these lost recipes and reintroducing them at weddings. By consulting with elders, using traditional cooking methods, and sourcing authentic ingredients, chefs are bringing back dishes that tell a story of times gone by. These culinary treasures not only add uniqueness to the wedding menu but also connect the guests with their roots.

Modern Takes on Classic Dishes

Modernising classic dishes isn't about erasing history; it's about adapting and reimagining the traditions for the current generation. Chefs are creatively playing with presentation, texture, and flavours, infusing old recipes with new twists. Think of a deconstructed samosa served as a gourmet appetiser or a fusion dessert combining gulab jamun with cheesecake. These reinterpretations allow the old and new to coexist harmoniously, preserving the essence while embracing innovation.

Serving Traditions: Ritualistic Foods in Indian Weddings

Food at Indian weddings isn't just about taste; it's woven into the rituals and traditions that make the celebration complete. Many weddings still serve specific dishes linked to religious or cultural practices. For instance, the inclusion of 'Panakam' in South Indian weddings, a sweet drink made of jaggery and spices, or 'Pithe' in Bengali weddings, a traditional rice cake. Including these ritualistic foods enriches the experience, creating a tangible link between the wedding and the deeper cultural significance.

Showcasing Regional Flavours and Dishes

India is a land of diverse cuisines, and each region has its own unique flavours and dishes. What better occasion than a wedding to showcase this richness? By featuring regional specialities, couples can give guests a culinary tour of India. From Kashmiri Wazwan to Kerala's Sadya, the possibilities are endless. This approach not only delights the palate but also educates guests about the vast culinary landscape of India.

The resurgence of traditional Indian wedding cuisine extends beyond being a mere trend; it represents a jubilant tribute to culinary heritage—a harmonious fusion of bygone eras and the present culinary landscape. It serves as a delectable vehicle for sharing culture, cherished memories, and profound love. By incorporating these captivating flavours, the wedding feast gains depth and imbues a lasting impression, making it as unforgettable as the special day itself.

A Table for Thousands: When Wedding Guests Overflow

Before we conclude the nuances of arranging a grand wedding feast, I'm reminded of a particularly intense episode that unfolded under the grandeur of Bangalore's palace skies. We were riding high on excitement, our spirits as lofty as the grand halls, awaiting the arrival of some 2000 to 2500 guests. A menu to dazzle the senses had been crafted with love from a caterer all the way from Hyderabad, and the aroma of the feast was enough to draw a crowd twice that size.

As the evening sparkled into life and the buffet beckoned, a sea of faces, far more than we anticipated, began to converge upon the dining area. It was a spectacle of enthusiasm as if the dishes laid out were casting a spell, pulling people into an eager dance around the banquet tables. The situation quickly escalated from bustling to overflowing, with guests flocking to the spread with an intensity that left us all a bit breathless.

Caught in this unexpected wave, we made a split-second decision to contain the swell. Closing off the dining area became an impromptu measure of crowd control, a dam to temper the human current. We wanted everyone to enjoy their meal as intended—savouring each bite, not merely rushing through it. Once guests had their fill, we allowed more to stream in, pacing the experience much like a well-conducted fest.

The threat of a stampede was a sobering undercurrent to the night's excitement, yet through quick thinking and a dash of resourcefulness, we skirted disaster. The caterer, a maestro in his own right, whipped up additional portions, and order was restored.

This experience served as a potent reminder that a wedding feast is not just about the food; it encompasses the entire experience of dining, the comfort of the guests, and the assurance that there's enough to go around. The importance of security arrangements and crowd control measures

crystallised before us. It was a lesson in humility and the need for flexibility, even in the face of the most careful planning.

Feasting together has always been at the heart of human connection, and in the grand celebration of a wedding, the food served is an expression of love, culture, creativity, and unity. Crafting a drool-worthy menu that caters to diverse palates while reviving and reimagining traditional dishes is no small feat. It's an art that can transform the wedding into an unforgettable culinary experience. Here's to a wedding feast that lingers in memories long after the last bite has been savoured and the last toast has been raised!

Chapter 10

Invitations and Return Gifts

Ah, the invitation—the very first taste your guests will get of your big day! Think about it: in the hustle and bustle of everyday life, when that gorgeous envelope lands in their hands or that artistic e-invite pops up on their screen, you've got their attention. This is where the magic begins. The colours, the script, the little design elements—they're all whispers of the grand celebration to come. But wait, that's not all. What about those thoughtful return gifts, those cultural treasures that say, "Hey, we're glad you were with us!" Now, that's a way to make a wedding memorable. Are you excited? So are we! Let's dive into the world of crafting invitations that sing and gifts that embrace, and let's make this chapter of your wedding planning a journey of creative joy!

Choosing a Theme and Colour Scheme:

A harmonious colour scheme and a unique theme lay down the red carpet, beckoning your guests into the world of your wedding. Are you envisioning a fairytale romance with soft pastels or a dramatic masquerade with deep, mysterious hues? Perhaps a seaside love affair with shades of blue? The colours and themes you select are not just artistic choices; they're a declaration of your style, setting the ambiance for every moment that follows. So, dig deep into your soul, pick a palette that sings, and craft a theme that echoes with your wedding's essence.

Crafting the Wording:

Ah, the words! Here's where your voice takes centre stage, where the ink dances to your love's rhythm. The language of your invitation must be more than proper etiquette and fancy fonts. It must resonate, be it through poetic verses that make hearts flutter or cheeky lines that draw a smile. Formal or casual, whimsical or reverent, the words should be uniquely you. After all, your love story is like no other, so why should your invitation sound ordinary? Guide your guests through the celebration's tone and nature with your choice of words, from the ceremonious invitation to the playful RSVP. Make them feel the excitement, the romance, the promise.

Integrating Cultural and Personal Touches:

The heart of an invitation is not just in its aesthetics but in the personality that it exudes. It's not merely an announcement; it's an embrace. Integrating elements that speak to your culture, your shared hobbies, or even your quirks can turn an invite into a cherished keepsake. Add a symbol that resonates

with your heritage, a quote that inspired your love, or even a sketch that tells a memorable story. Make it a window to your world, a reflection of your union. It's these seemingly minute details that warm the hearts and remind everyone that they are part of a love that's genuine and profound.

Quality and Sustainability:

The tactile sensation of the paper, the elegance of the print, the finesse of the envelope—all these elements whisper a promise of what's to come. But quality doesn't mean forgetting our Earth. Many couples today are intertwining elegance with responsibility, choosing recycled paper or ink that leaves a softer footprint. Some even go for plantable cards that bloom into flowers, a poetic testament to a love that grows and nurtures. It's not just a trend; it's a statement that love and care extend beyond the couple to the world they inhabit. In a world craving for sustainability, let your invitation be a testament to a future filled with love, care, and respect for the environment.

An invitation is merely the opening act of the grand theatre that celebrates your love. Each guest is a cherished participant, and every moment is a treasured memory. Watch as it unravels, a symphony of beauty, authenticity, and grace, resonating with the enchanting anticipation of what awaits in the future.

Chapter 11

Wedding Management Maestros

Wedding planners are more than just coordinators; they are the architects of dreams. They not only help conceptualise and visualise the wedding but also take care of the meticulous details that make the day unique and special. They handle the logistical aspects of the event, such as coordinating vendors, managing timelines, overseeing the budget, and ensuring that everything runs smoothly on the wedding day. Wedding planners act as the central point of contact for all wedding-related matters, troubleshooting issues as they arise and making sure every detail is executed as envisioned.

What's the difference between a Wedding Planner and a Wedding Designer, then? A wedding designer is a professional focused on the aesthetic and thematic elements of a wedding. They conceptualise and design the visual components, from decor and colour palettes to lighting and table arrangements. Wedding designers work closely with couples to define the look and feel of the event, ensuring that the venue and its decorations reflect the couple's personal style and vision. They collaborate with other vendors, such as florists and rental companies, to bring the desired ambiance to life.

Below are some of the key responsibilities that set them apart:

Vendor Coordination: From selecting the right caterers and photographers to entertainment, a wedding planner's connections in the industry can be invaluable. They help negotiate contracts, manage timelines, and ensure that every vendor is aligned with the wedding's theme and vision.

Logistical Management: This involves planning and coordinating the flow of the wedding day. They manage everything from transportation for guests to the timeline of the ceremony and reception, ensuring that everything runs smoothly and according to plan.

Budgeting and Financial Planning: One of the most daunting aspects of planning a wedding can be the budget. Wedding planners are trained to help couples create realistic budgets, track expenses, and find creative solutions to make the most of their financial resources.

Guest Management: Coordinating guest arrivals, accommodations, transport, and special needs are part of the planner's responsibilities. They help in creating seating charts, handling RSVPs, and ensuring that all guests are cared for.

Timeline Construction: A planner builds a comprehensive timeline that schedules each element of the wedding day, ensuring that nothing overlaps or conflicts. They make sure that every moment, from the bride's makeup to the last dance, is perfectly timed.

Problem-Solving and Crisis Management: No matter how well everything is planned, unexpected issues may arise. Wedding planners are equipped to handle these unexpected twists and turns, be it last-minute changes or emergencies, with grace and efficiency.

A wedding planner often becomes a confidant and emotional support system, too. They provide a listening ear and professional advice, helping to alleviate stress and allow the couple to enjoy the process.

Styles and Themes: How Designers Shape the Event

The style and theme of a wedding create the ambiance and set the tone for the celebration. Wedding Designers are masters at crafting and curating this essential aspect. Here's how they contribute:

- ## Understanding the Couple's Vision

Designers take the time to sit down with the couple and truly understand their desires and dreams. They consider the couple's personalities, their love story, and their cultural backgrounds, weaving these into a theme that's both personal and unique.

- ## Trend Awareness

Being constantly immersed in the world of weddings, designers are up-to-date with the latest trends and can recommend styles that are fashionable yet timeless. They might suggest seasonal colours, contemporary decor ideas, or even interactive experiences that resonate with the modern guest.

- ## Customised Solutions

No two weddings are the same, and wedding designers pride themselves on creating tailored solutions. They collaborate with decorators and other vendors to produce a visual experience that's aligned with the couple's vision, down to the tiniest detail.

- ## Harmonising Elements

From invitations to table settings, from the venue's decor to the food presentation, planners ensure a coherent and harmonious expression of the theme throughout every aspect

of the wedding. They orchestrate a symphony of visuals and experiences that feels seamless and integrated.

Selecting the Right Wedding Planner

Selecting the ideal wedding planner is akin to discovering the perfect dance partner for the most exquisite waltz of your life. The connection, understanding, and trust must be there, guiding you effortlessly through each step, twirl, and dip. A wedding planner's role goes beyond mere organisation; they are the architects of dreams, the conductors of emotions, and the artists painting your love story. In this section, we'll explore how to select the one who resonates with your vision and turns it into a harmonious reality.

Identifying Your Needs: A Checklist for Couples

Before embarking on the journey to find your wedding planner, it's essential to have a clear understanding of what you want and need. Here's how you can prepare:

- **Determine the Level of Service:** Are you looking for full-service planning, partial planning, or just day-of coordination? Your decision should align with your expectations, budget, and the time you can dedicate to planning.
- **Define Your Style and Vision:** Know what themes, styles, and elements you desire in your wedding. A

planner who specialises in your preferred style can bring your vision to life more effectively.

- **Consider Your Personality and Preferences:** Do you prefer a planner who is more hands-on or one who seeks your input at every step? Your compatibility with a planner's working style is crucial.

Researching and Interviewing: Finding the Perfect Fit

Once you've outlined your needs, the next step is researching and interviewing potential planners:

- **Conduct Thorough Research:** Look at online reviews, portfolios, and social media presence, and ask for references. It can give you a sense of their style, experience, and reputation.

- **Arrange Face-to-Face Interviews:** Meeting planners in person or via video calls allows you to gauge chemistry and compatibility. It's an opportunity to ask questions, discuss expectations, and feel their passion and professionalism.

- **Review Their Proposal and Contract:** Take the time to go through their detailed proposal and contract. Ensure that it covers all aspects of their service, including their fees, cancellation policy, and any other important terms and conditions.

- **Listen to Your Instincts:** Sometimes, the connection with a planner just feels right. Trusting your gut feeling can lead you to the planner who truly resonates with your vision and personality.

The right planner becomes not just a service provider but a friend, confidante, and the maestro who orchestrates your love's perfect symphony.

Wedding Planner

- Brainstorming
- Budgeting
- Vendor filtering
- Scheduling appointment
- Approving design
- Follow up
- Rundown making
- Vendor technical meeting
- Family technical meeting
- D day execution

The Bigger Picture: How Planners Impact the Entire Celebration

Wedding planners are like the talented directors of a blockbuster movie. They possess the vision, coordinate the crew, ensure perfect timing, and execute the masterpiece with finesse. Their impact is extensive, spanning from the initial concept discussion to the final dance of the night. Let's explore how planners influence and elevate the entire celebration:

Stress Reduction: Leaving the Worry to the Professionals

One of the most significant advantages of hiring a wedding planner is the reduction of stress.

- **Expert Guidance:** Planners provide professional expertise, ensuring that every detail is managed with precision. They anticipate potential problems and find solutions even before they arise.

- **Time Management:** Wedding planning requires countless hours of work. A planner takes on this burden, freeing the couple to enjoy the engagement period without the stress of deadlines and decisions.

- **A Buffer in Tricky Situations:** Whether negotiating with vendors or managing sensitive family dynamics, having a planner as an intermediary can keep the peace and reduce stress.

- **Peace of Mind:** Knowing that a professional is handling the logistics gives couples the confidence to relax and enjoy their special day, focusing on each other and their guests.

Creating a Seamless Experience: From Rehearsals to Reception

A planner's work goes beyond the wedding day; they create a seamless experience throughout the entire wedding journey.

- **Cohesive Vision:** Planners ensure that all elements – from invitations to decor – align with the chosen theme, creating a unified and cohesive experience for the guests.

- **Managing Rehearsals:** They orchestrate the wedding rehearsal, making sure everyone knows their roles, timing, and positions, setting the stage for a smooth ceremony.

- **Coordinating Vendors:** Planners act as the point of contact for all vendors, aligning their schedules and requirements to ensure that everything runs like clockwork.

- **On-the-Day Execution:** On the wedding day, they manage everything from setup to the flow of events, ensuring that everything proceeds without a hitch.

- **Post-Wedding Support:** Whether handling returns, managing rentals, or providing assistance with thank-you notes, planners often continue their support even after the wedding day.

Wedding Planning Services List

Wedding Planning   Food and Beverage   Wedding Styling

Photography   Find a venue for your wedding day   Wedding Decoration

Chapter 12

Tying Up Loose Ends

As the wedding day approaches, the excitement builds, and so does the realisation that there are still many details to finalise. Let's talk about that last dash to the finish line, shall we? This isn't about setting off alarm bells; it's about dotting the i's and crossing the t's, ensuring your big day unfolds just like you've envisioned.

Last-Minute Checklist

1. **Confirming Vendors:** Give your vendors a buzz. A little nudge to make sure you're all singing from the same song sheet can save you from a world of "I thought you..." moments. From the florist to the caterer and the photographer! A quick catch-up can keep things peachy.

2. **Finalising Guest List:** Got your RSVPs all tallied up? Great! Now, share that golden list with the folks who need it. This isn't just about who gets chicken or fish; it's about perfecting that seating chart and ensuring no one is stuck behind a pillar.

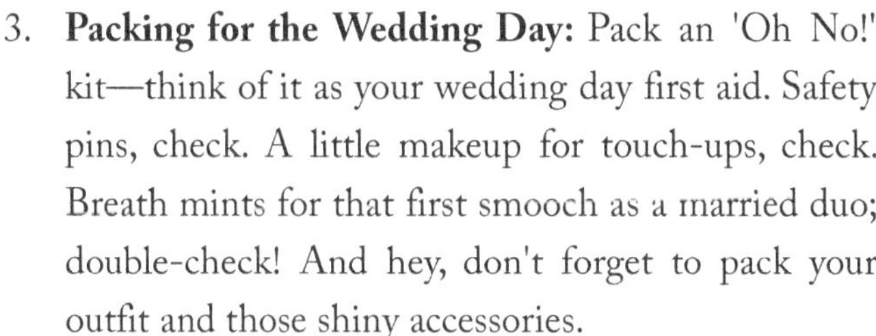

3. **Packing for the Wedding Day:** Pack an 'Oh No!' kit—think of it as your wedding day first aid. Safety pins, check. A little makeup for touch-ups, check. Breath mints for that first smooch as a married duo; double-check! And hey, don't forget to pack your outfit and those shiny accessories.

4. **Rehearsing:** Whether it's a walk down the aisle or a special dance, practice makes perfect. Schedule final rehearsals for anything that needs coordination. Let's make it flawless.

5. **Distributing Responsibilities:** It's like assembling your very own wedding avengers. Choose your most reliable pals or family members to take charge of little missions – helping the guests, herding those precious gifts to safety, you name it. Sharing the load means you get to be the VIP of your party, not the head honcho of chores.

6. **Spa and Beauty Appointments:** That last-minute mani-pedi or the oh-so-relaxing facial shouldn't be skipped. It's not just about looking fabulous, but feeling serene and spa-tastic, too.

7. **Licence and Legal Documents:** Legal stuff – it's like the homework of weddings, but hey, no pass without it! Double-check those documents, licences, and all the paper jazz to ensure you're officially official when it's time to tie the knot.

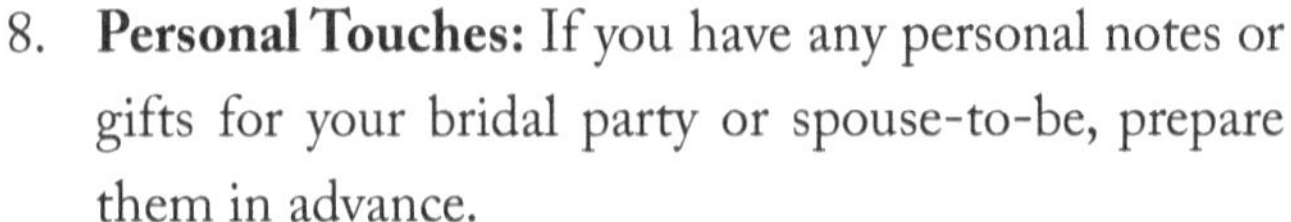

8. **Personal Touches:** If you have any personal notes or gifts for your bridal party or spouse-to-be, prepare them in advance.

9. **Payment and Gratuities:** Last but not least, let's talk money and sense. Get those envelopes stuffed with the agreed moolah for your vendors—and don't forget a little extra something for their tip-top service.

Stick to this game plan, and you'll waltz into your wedding day all smiles and stress-free, ready to soak up every beautiful moment.

Wedding PLANNING

- ♡ Set Date and Location
- ♡ Set a Budget
- ♡ Create a Guest List
- ♡ Find Vendors
- ♡ Plan Events
- ♡ Choose a Wedding Dress
- ♡ Decoration and Theme
- ♡ Invitations and RSVPs
- ♡ Plan Meals and Drinks
- ♡ Souvenirs and Gifts
- ♡ Transport Arrangements
- ♡ Honeymoon Planning

Mental Well-being and Dealing with Stress

The quiet before a wedding is a mix of emotions – there's laughter and excitement about the future but also moments of anxiety. This is true in Ayesha's story, especially during the busy wedding preparations. Just before her entrance at the Nikah ceremony, she was suddenly overwhelmed with panic. Then, without warning, the weight of 'forever' pressed down on her. In her dressing room, she found herself in the throes of a fear so raw and overwhelming that it spilt from her eyes, smudging her carefully done makeup. Her family gathered around in a whirlwind of worry, but their well-meaning presence felt more like a crowd to her panicked heart.

It was her uncles, with their gentle ways, who became her unexpected anchors. They sat with her, they did not attempt to hush her fears. Instead, they patiently heard them. They reminded her of the life she would build and not of the life she would leave behind. Their words were like a balm and slowly, Ayesha's sobs gave way to quiet nods and then to a shy smile that marked the beginning of her healing and her walk forward.

Ayesha's story isn't just about a bride overcoming cold feet; it's a poignant note on the importance of mental well-being amidst the clamour of wedding bells. It's a call to remember that behind the perfect veneer of wedding plans, genuine human emotions pulse, deserving of attention.

So, in the canvas of checklists and schedules, let's not forget to draw in moments for stillness and support. Surrounding yourself with loved ones and those who genuinely support you can make all the difference. Lean on them, share your feelings, and don't hesitate to delegate tasks. Trust others to take care of things, and remember that letting go of control can be a liberating experience.

Incorporate self-care into your routine. Whether it's meditation, yoga, or simply indulging in hobbies you enjoy, these activities can keep you grounded and calm. Open and honest communication with your partner, family, and planners can prevent misunderstandings, keeping everyone aligned and in harmony.

If stress does become unmanageable, professional assistance such as counselling or therapy can provide valuable support. Sometimes, an objective perspective can help you navigate the whirlwind of wedding preparations.

Prepare yourself for the emotional transition that marriage brings. If you feel you may become overly emotional, create a support strategy with someone who can be there for you. And most importantly, allow yourself to laugh, make mistakes, and genuinely enjoy the process.

Balancing the practical aspects of planning with emotional well-being leads to a more fulfilling and meaningful celebration. Love, joy, connection, and a touch of

self-care – these are the ingredients for a mentally healthy and heartwarming wedding experience.

Handling Emergencies and Unexpected Hiccups

No matter how meticulously planned a wedding is, unexpected situations can arise. It's the grace with which these are handled that can set the tone for a remarkable event.

On that note, I recollect a splendid scene: the sky ablaze with hues of orange and pink as the stage was set for one of the grandest weddings of my early career. With anticipation bubbling within me, I watched as the last few touches were added to the outdoor setting with a pathway adorned with fifty tastefully sourced chandeliers, promising a walk to remember. Guests would arrive in a mere three hours, and the atmosphere was filled with excitement.

However, Mother Nature had other plans. Without warning, the skies opened up, unleashing unforgiving winds paired with torrential rain. The beautifully laid pathway became a casualty, and the chandeliers became a shattered dream. With the destruction laid bare before my eyes, panic was a natural intruder, but time was not a luxury I could afford.

In those moments, dismay had to give way to determination. With no time to dwell on the misfortune, I had to think on my feet. The pathway to matrimonial bliss might have been disrupted, but the journey could not end there. With deft decision-making and an unyielding spirit, I spearheaded the

team to forge a new entrance, transforming the calamity into an opportunity to showcase our resilience and creativity. Meanwhile, the outdoor decor—once meant to revel under the stars—found a new home indoors, and its charm was redefined.

Those two frantic hours taught me an invaluable lesson—the imperative need for a backup plan. The incident etched in me the realisation that while nature's script is unwritten, our preparation for its unpredictability must be meticulous. It highlights the essential aspects of planning ahead to tackle emergencies and underscores the need to be ever-vigilant and adaptive.

1. **Creating a Backup Plan:** Outdoor shindig? Stunning, but let's whisper about the 'what ifs.' Chat with your venue about a plan B for rain, shine, or anything in between. It's like an umbrella for your wedding plans – you might not need it, but boy, does it feel good to have it!

2. **Vendor No-show or Issues:** Ensure that you have all your vendors' emergency contact numbers. But let's also have a quick-draw pal who can leap into action if one of your wedding superheroes runs into trouble. It's like having a wedding sidekick for your sidekicks.

3. **Medical Emergencies:** A little kit of 'fix-its' should be within arm's reach. Because tripping down the aisle should only happen in rom-coms, not at your wedding.

4. **Wardrobe Malfunctions:** A popped button or a stubborn zipper shouldn't be the villain of the day. Keep a mini sewing kit stashed with someone who can stitch or pin in a pinch.

5. **Last-minute Guest Changes:** Whether it's unexpected plus-ones or cancellations, having a flexible seating plan and informing the catering staff can solve this hiccup.

6. **Technical Difficulties:** If you're relying on technology for any part of the ceremony or reception, such as slideshows or special music, make sure there's a tech-savvy person on hand to handle any unexpected issues.

7. **Emotional Support:** Nerves? Totally normal. But let's have a zen guru in your corner. This is the person who can soothe, calm, and collect you faster than you can say "I do." They're the human version of a deep breath and a warm hug.

8. **Lost or Forgotten Items:** Keep a list of essential items and double-check them. If something is forgotten, have a plan for how to get it or who to call.

9. **Financial Readiness:** Sometimes, the unexpected pops up and it's usually waving a price tag. Keep a little extra cash or a credit card handy for those last-minute lifesavers, like a sudden need for extra rides or that one extra box of tissues.

Embracing the unexpected doesn't mean leaving things to chance; it means being prepared for the possibilities and maintaining a positive attitude. Having strategies in place can turn potential disasters into mere bumps in the road, allowing the focus to remain on the joy and significance of the occasion.

A Timeline for the Big Day

Every second counts on the wedding day, and having a carefully crafted timeline ensures that everything flows smoothly. But where to begin?

Start with the milestones—the ceremony, the reception, those moments steeped in tradition. Now, plan backwards. Give yourself generous slots to get ready, arrive in style, and, of course, spend a few precious minutes just to catch your breath.

Hair and makeup are up next. It's not just you; your bridal party will also need time in the styling chair. And it almost always takes a bit longer than you'd think. Planning photos before the ceremony? Pad in some extra time there, too, so you're not rushing those once-in-a-lifetime shots.

Mealtime—particularly breakfast—is crucial. It's a marathon, not a sprint, and you'll want the energy. Then, make sure everyone who is important has a copy of this schedule. This isn't just about you; it's about creating a smooth experience for all.

And who'll make sure this all ticks along nicely? Your wedding planner, if you have one, or a trusty relative who's got an eye for detail and timing. They'll be the conductor of your day, keeping the tempo, so you can lose yourself in the celebration, not the schedule.

Things might run late, and that's okay. Embrace the flow of the day and enjoy every moment. The timeline is there to support you, not constrain you. Enjoy the ride, knowing that you've prepared well, and let the day unfold in its unique and beautiful way.

Enjoying Your Day to the Fullest

The wedding day is a culmination of dreams, a tapestry woven with love, commitment, family, and joy. It transcends the decorations, sumptuous food, stunning attire, and meticulously planned details. This book has been your guide, confidant, and partner in crafting the perfect celebration. It demystifies complexities, guides you through decisions, and stands beside you as you make this day uniquely yours.

From early-morning rituals to late-night dances, every moment is a treasure. The laughter, tears, promises, and cheers are the true jewels of this day. Together, we've explored each aspect, delved into traditions, weighed choices, and arrived at this moment, ready and resplendent.

As the couple stands on the threshold of a new chapter, it's a time to pause and be present. To revel in the love that has guided, the support that has strengthened, and the shared dreams that have led.

In the whirlwind, it's spontaneous laughter, unexpected hugs, impromptu dances, and honest, heartfelt words that linger in memory. These are the moments this book has helped craft, unscripted and pure, capturing the soul of your celebration.

This vibrant day, filled with emotions, is not just a beginning but a beautiful milestone. It's a testament to growing love, overcoming challenges, and a future sparkling with possibilities.

As the music winds down and night wraps its arms around the tired but happy couple, they step forward together, hearts full, paths aligned, and spirits soaring. The wedding day ends, but the adventure begins, and this book's pages will remain a companion, a reminder of the love, laughter, and planning that made it possible.

Remember, planning a wedding is a journey, not a race. If the path ahead seems daunting, seek expert guidance. A wedding planner can be your trusted ally, ensuring every detail reflects your unique love story.

Here's to love, laughter, and happily ever after. May your wedding be everything you've dreamed of and more.